NEW National Cu Mathematics 3

K. M. Vickers
M. J. Tipler
H. L. van Hiele

© K. M. Vickers, M. J. Tipler and H. L. van Hiele 1991, 1995

First published in 1994 by Canterbury Educational Ltd
Reprinted 1994
Revised edition published in 1995 by:
Stanley Thornes (Publishers) Ltd
Ellenborough House, Wellington Street
CHELTENHAM, Glos. GL50 1YD
England

A catalogue record for this book is available from the British Library

ISBN 1-873941-25-0
ISBN 1-873941-26-9 (with answers)

Printed and bound in Great Britain by
BPC Paulton Books Ltd, Paulton

PREFACE

"National Curriculum Mathematics" by K.M. Vickers and M.J. Tipler is a complete course carefully designed and now updated to ensure full coverage of the revised National Curriculum.

In the 1995 revised National Curriculum, the Level Descriptions describe the performance that pupils working at a particular level should demonstrate. This book covers all the material in Level 3 of the National Curriculum in three separate sections: Number; Shape, Space and Measures; and Handling Data. Using and Applying Mathematics is integrated throughout the book. The material is presented in this order to enable pupils, or a group of pupils, to work across the different areas of mathematics at different levels.

Each section begins with revision from previous levels, printed on pink paper for ease of identification. Each section ends with a review chapter which contains revision questions on the material developed in this book. In each of the other chapters, every skill developing exercise finishes with review questions.

With the exception of Review chapters, all chapters begin with "Look Around You At . . ." which is an introduction to the chapter and encourages pupils to relate the topic to everyday experiences. These chapters end with "Work This Out". Throughout each topic, relevance to everyday life is emphasised. The acquisition of knowledge and skills is integrated with the use and application of these skills and knowledge.

This book does not replace the teacher. Rather, it is a resource for both the pupil and the teacher. The teacher can be flexible about what is taught and when.

Throughout the book there is a variety of activities: skill developing exercises, investigations, practical work, problem solving activities, discussion exercises, puzzles and games. All the activities are related to the topic being studied. Whenever possible, activities and exercises have been written as open rather than closed tasks.

There is a good balance between tasks which develop knowledge, skills and understanding, and those which develop the ability to tackle and solve problems. Many activities do both. There is a thorough and careful development of each topic. Questions within each exercise or activity are carefully graded to build pupil confidence.

This book takes into consideration:
> pupils' needs
> pupils' interests
> pupils' experiences
> the need for pupils to explore mathematics
> the use of technology
> both independent and co-operative work habits

This book encourages pupils to:
> use a wide range of mathematics
> discuss mathematical ideas
> undertake investigations
> participate in practical activities
> relate mathematics to everyday life
> select appropriate methods for a task
> communicate information
> discuss difficulties
> ask questions

It is hoped that the pupil who uses this book will:
> develop a real interest in mathematics
> become well motivated
> gain much enjoyment from mathematics
> develop a fascination with mathematics
> develop an ability to use mathematics in other subjects
> become confident in the use of the calculator and computer
> gain a firm foundation for further study
> become proficient at applying mathematics to everyday life
> develop both independent and co-operative work habits
> become aware of the power and purpose of mathematics
> develop an ability to communicate mathematics
> develop an appreciation of the relevance of mathematics
> develop an ability to think precisely, logically and creatively
> become confident at mathematics
> gain a sense of satisfaction

Calculator keying sequences are appropriate for most calculators.

The version of LOGO used is LOGOTRON – standard LOGO for the BBC.

K.M. Vickers
M.J. Tipler

Acknowledgements

The authors wish to thank all those firms and enterprises who have so kindly given permission to reproduce tables and other material. A special thanks to S. Bennett for her valuable contribution; to Rob Henderson for the illustrations and J. McClelland for the photographs.

Every effort has been made to trace all the copyright holders. If any have been inadvertently overlooked the publishers will be pleased to make the necessary arrangement at the first opportunity.

Contents

NUMBER

SHAPE, SPACE and MEASURES

HANDLING DATA

Level Descriptions for Level 3

Attainment Target 1: Using and Applying Mathematics

■ Level 3

Pupils try different approaches and find ways of overcoming difficulties that arise when they are solving problems. They are beginning to organise their work and check results. Pupils discuss their mathematical work and are beginning to explain their thinking. They use and interpret mathematical symbols and diagrams. Pupils show that they understand a general statement by finding particular examples that match it.

Attainment Target 2: Number

■ Level 3

Pupils show understanding of place value in numbers up to 1000 and use this to make approximations. They have begun to use decimal notation and to recognise negative numbers, in contexts such as money, temperature and calculator displays. Pupils use mental recall of addition and subtraction facts to 20 in solving problems involving larger numbers. They use mental recall of the 2, 5 and 10 multiplication tables, and others up to 5×5, in solving whole-number problems involving multiplication or division, including those that give rise to remainders. Pupils use calculator methods where numbers include several digits. They have begun to develop mental strategies, and use them to find methods for adding and subtracting numbers with at least two digits.

Attainment Target 3: Shape, Space and Measures

■ Level 3

Pupils classify 3-D and 2-D shapes in various ways using mathematical properties such as reflective symmetry. They use non-standard units and standard metric units of length, capacity, mass and time, in a range of contexts.

Attainment Target 4: Handling Data

■ Level 3

Pupils extract and interpret information presented in simple tables and lists. They construct bar charts and pictograms, where the symbol represents a group of units, to communicate information they have gathered, and they interpret information presented to them in these forms.

NUMBER

Number from Previous Levels

ADDING AND SUBTRACTING

The **addition facts** on this table should be known.

+	0	1	2	3	4	5	6	7	8	9	10
0	0	1	2	3	4	5	6	7	8	9	10
1	1	2	3	4	5	6	7	8	9	10	
2	2	3	4	5	6	7	8	9	10		
3	3	4	5	6	7	8	9	10			
4	4	5	6	7	8	9	10				
5	5	6	7	8	9	10					

The facts on this table can be used to do subtraction.

$$4 + 6 = 10$$
$$\text{so} \quad 10 - 6 = 4$$
$$\text{and} \quad 10 - 4 = 6$$

READING and WRITING NUMBERS

We read 432 as four hundred and thirty two.

Fifty six is written as 56.
Eight hundred and two is written as 802.

In numbers like 56, 32 and 12 the first number is the **tens** number.

In 56 there are 5 tens.   In 32 there are 3 tens.
In 12 there is 1 ten.

continued . . .

. . . from previous page

HALVES AND QUARTERS

Half of these cats are shaded. One half is written as $\frac{1}{2}$.

One quarter of these apples are red. One quarter is written as $\frac{1}{4}$.

PATTERNS

Sometimes we can find a **pattern** that repeats.

Examples

3, 2, 1, 3, 2, 1, 3, 2, 1

Often we can work out how to carry the pattern on. If we were asked to write down the next 3 numbers for the number pattern above, we would write 3, 2, 1.

continued . . .

. . . from previous page

We can find many patterns when we add and subtract.

4 + 0 = 4	7 − 6 = 1
4 + 1 = 5	7 − 5 = 2
4 + 2 = 6	7 − 4 = 3
4 + 3 = 7	7 − 3 = 4 and so on

The **even** numbers are 2, 4, 6, 8, 10, 12 and so on.

The **odd** numbers are 1, 3, 5, 7, 9, 11 and so on.

We can use a **symbol** like ■ or ● or ★ to stand for a missing number.

If 4 + ● = 10, then ● must stand for 6.
This is because 4 + 6 = 10.

If we are given the pattern 1, 3, 5, ■, 9, then ■ would stand for 7.

REVISION EXERCISE

1. Brenna has 4 pencils.

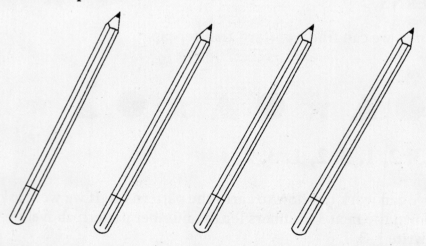

If her friend gave her 3 more pencils, how many would she have then?

2. Sam has two piles of counters.

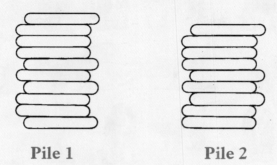

Pile 1   Pile 2

(a) How many counters are in pile 1?

(b) How many counters are in pile 2?

(c) Which pile has more counters?

(d) If the counters were put beside each other in a line, which pile would make the longer line?

3. Pam was painting a pattern on one of the stalls at the school fair. Copy this pattern and draw the next three shapes.

4. Write down what the next two lines would be.

(a) $3 + 0 = 3$
  $3 + 1 = 4$
  $3 + 2 = 5$

(b) $5 - 0 = 5$
  $5 - 1 = 4$
  $5 - 2 = 3$

(c) $6 = 5 + 1$
  $6 = 4 + 2$
  $6 = 3 + 3$

5.

Copy these sentences. Fill in the gaps with one of these

more   fewer   the same number of   than   as

(a) There are _____ horses _____ cats.

(b) There are _____ horses _____ dogs.

(c) There are _____ cats _____ horses.

(d) There are _____ dogs _____ cats.

(e) There are _____ cats _____ dogs.

6. Write in numbers.

   (a) Twenty seven

   (b) Fifty six

   (c) Three hundred and forty two

   (d) Four hundred and two

7. Find the missing number.

   (a) $3 + \blacktriangle = 5$

   (b) $6 - \bullet = 1$

   (c) $\blacksquare + 5 = 9$

   (d) $8 - \bullet = 8$

   (e) $7 = \blacktriangle + 3$

   (f) $9 - \blacksquare = 3$

8. Winstone is asked to colour one half of these boxes red. How many would be red?

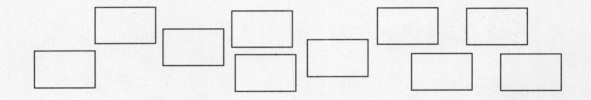

9. What could ★ stand for?

   (a) 2, 4, 6, 8, ★, 12

   (b) 7, 9, 11, ★, 15, 17

   (c) 1, 2, 2, 3, 3, 3, ★, 4, 4, 4

10. Peter and Catherine were playing a game. In the game two dice were tossed and the numbers added. What is Peter's total?

15

11. Write down the next 3 numbers.

    (a) 1, 2, 1, 2, 1, 2,   (b) 4, 3, 2, 1, 4, 3, 2, 1, 4,

12. A street has houses with numbers from 1 to 25.

    (a) How many houses have even numbers?

    (b) How many houses have odd numbers?

13. Find

    (a) 3 + 2   (b) 3 + 6   (c) 2 + 8   (d) 4 + 6   (e) 2 + 7

    (f) 10 – 5   (g) 5 – 3   (h) 9 – 5   (i) 8 – 5   (j) 4 – 3

    (k) 9 – 9   (l) 4 – 0   (m) 10 – 1

14.

Dianne had 8 counters. Amy took 3. How many would Dianne have left?

15. Draw 8 triangles like this one.

    Colour one quarter of them.

    How many have you coloured?

16. 5 + 3 = 8. What other numbers add to 8?

17. Draw the two shapes that could be on the dotted lines to finish the pattern.

    (a) ■ ▴ ■ ▴ ▴ ■ ▴ ■ ▴ ▴ ■ ▴ __ __ ▴ ■ ▴

    (b) ● ● ▴ S ● ● ▴ S ● __ __ S

    (c) ● ◯ ● ● ◯ ◯ ◯ ● ◯ ◯ ● ● __ __ ● ◯

18. Mary bought a 5p and a 6p stamp. She paid for these with 20p. How much change did she get?

19. James said "I subtracted two numbers. They were both less than 10 and I got an answer of 2." Write down all the subtractions James could have done.

20. What coins would you be likely to use to pay for these?

(a)    (b)

21. 6 + 3 = 9. What other numbers add to 9?

22.

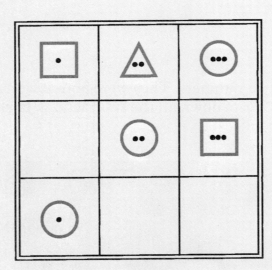

Copy this box. Draw shapes in the empty squares to finish the pattern.

23. How many tens are there in

    (a) 92   (b) 40   (c) 12   (d) 4?

24. ● + ● = ★.

   ● is a number between 0 and 10. ★ is also a number between 0 and 10. Find what numbers ● and ★ could be.

25. Find two ways of carrying this pattern on.

Look Around You at . . .

Magazines and Newspapers

Deane breaks City hearts

Leeds 3 Man City 2

MANCHESTER CITY were shattered by an 85th-minute winner from Brian Deane after a two-goal fightback that had shaken a Leeds side who seemed to be coasting to victory.

City's cause looked to be lost as first-half goals from the in-form Rod Wallace and Gary Speed put Leeds in firm control after just 22 minutes.

But the introduction of substitute Carl Griffiths, a £500,000 signing from Shrewsbury, put new sparkle into City who reduced the deficit with a 20-yard cracker from Mike Sheron.

Griffiths levelled on the hour, before Deane's late winner broke City hearts.

PRACTICAL 1:1

Look in newspapers and magazines. Find as many numbers as you can to do with a sport or hobby that you like. You could choose one of the following:

| soccer | netball | hockey | gymnastics |

| swimming | music | reading |

Choose a way of showing your group what you found. You could make a poster or make up a story using the numbers.

DISCUSSION 1:2

● An abacus can be used to show numbers by putting beads on sticks.

3 is shown as

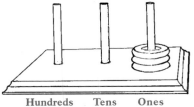

16 is shown as
(There is one bead on the tens and six beads on the ones.)

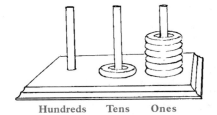

What do you think 562 would look like on an abacus? **Discuss** with your partner or group.

● Only 9 beads will fit on each stick of this abacus. Why? **Discuss.** The number 97 is shown on this abacus. **Discuss** what to do if you want to add one more bead to the tens stick.

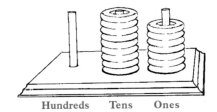

● This abacus has four sticks. **Discuss** what would be written under the new stick. How would you show the number 1876 on this abacus? **Discuss.**

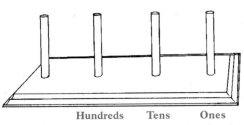

PLACE VALUE

The number 52 has 5 tens and 2 ones. The number 25 has 2 tens and 5 ones.
0, 1, 2, 3, 4, 5, 6, 7, 8 and 9 are called **digits**. The **place** of a digit tells us its **value**.

This chart shows **place value**.

Thousands	Hundreds	Tens	Units (or ones)
4	8	7	3

For instance, in the number 4873,   the digit 4 means 4 thousands
the digit 8 means 8 hundreds
the digit 7 means 7 tens
the digit 3 means 3 ones.

DISCUSSION 1:3

Rachel, Ashrak and Fiona were asked to write nine hundred and two in figures. This is what they wrote.

Rachel 92

Ashrack 9002

Fiona 902

Rachel said, "There are no tens so we don't have to put anything for them".
What might the others say? **Discuss.**
Who has written it the right way? **Discuss.**
How could you write nine thousand and two in figures? **Discuss.**

Worked Example (a) Write 5242 in words.

(b) Write one thousand four hundred and sixty five using digits.

Answer (a) There are 5 thousands, 2 hundreds, 4 tens and 2 ones so we write this as five thousand two hundred and forty two.

(b) We must have a 1 in the thousands place, a 4 in the hundreds place, a 6 in the tens place and a 5 in the ones place. We write this as 1465.

Worked Example What is the place value of 8 in these?

(a)

38

(b)

389

(c)

8039

Answer (a) In 38, the 8 is in the ones place. The place value of 8 is ones.

(b) In 389, the 8 is in the tens place. The place value of 8 is tens.

(c) In 8039, the 8 is in the thousands place. The place value of 8 is thousands.

EXERCISE 1:4

1. Write these in words.

(a) 24   (b) 16   (c) 240   (d) 204   (e) 362

(f) 2400   (g) 2962   (h) 2004   (i) 2040   (j) 3000

2. Use digits to write these.

   (a) ninety seven

   (b) two hundred and forty six

   (c) eight hundred and three

   (d) five hundred and ninety

   (e) one thousand two hundred
   and thirty three

   (f) four thousand nine hundred
   and three

   (g) two thousand and four

3. Write in figures.

   (a)
   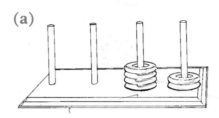

   (b)
   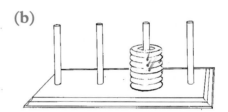

   (c)
   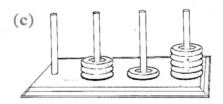

   (d)
   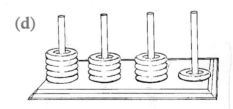

   (e)
   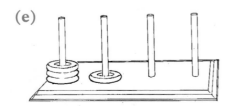

   (f)
   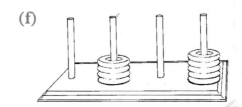

4. Copy the crossnumber and fill it in.

1.		2.		■	3.	4.	5.
	■	6.	7.		■	8.	
9.	10.			■	11.		
12.		■	13.	14.			■
■	15.	16.			■	17.	
18.			■	19.	20.		■
	■	21.					■

CLUES

ACROSS

1. 3 hundreds and 2 tens and 4 ones
3. 6 hundreds and 5 tens and 3 ones
6. 3 tens and 9 ones
8. Four tens
9. Eight thousand seven hundred and fifty one
11. Eighty one
12. Six tens
13. Five hundreds and seven tens and four ones
15. Four thousand two hundred and five
18. Nine hundred and four ones
19. Five hundred and thirty two
21. 8 thousands and 3 hundreds

DOWN

1. Three thousand and eighty six
2. Four hundreds and three tens and five ones
4. Five thousand four hundred and eighty four
5. 3 hundreds and 1 one
7. Nine thousands and one hundred and five tens
10. Seven thousand and forty
14. Seven thousand five hundred and fifty
16. Two hundreds and four tens and eight ones
17. One ten and two ones
18. Ninety six
20. Three tens

5. Which digit is in the tens place?

    (a) 432   (b) 8431   (c) 5006   (d) 4020   (e) 16

6. Which digit is in the hundreds place?

    (a) 8962   (b) 324   (c) 4032   (d) 5980   (e) 3000

7. Which digit is in the thousands place?

    (a) 4320   (b) 8004   (c) 6400   (d) 9302   (e) 700

    (f) 4870   (g) 7004   (h) 5700   (i) 7843   (j) 1070

8. What is the place value of the seven in each of these?

    (a) 7   (b) 72   (c) 837   (d) 796   (e) 8760

    (f) 4870   (g) 7004   (h) 5700   (i) 7843   (j) 1070

9. Two Australian visitors in Britain had only £100 notes, £10 notes and £1 coins in their bag. What notes and coins could they use to pay for the following?

    (a) a gold bracelet which cost £121

    (b) a ride in a balloon which cost £250

    (c) a plane ticket which cost £846

10. At the end of their holiday the Australian visitors had four £100 notes, eight £10 notes and fifteen £1 coins left. How much is this altogether?

Review 1   (a) Write 8092 in words.

(b) Write five thousand four hundred and two in figures.

Review 2   What is the place value of the 6 in the following?

(a) 6321   (b) 8060   (c) 506   (d) 7681

PRACTICAL 1:5

MAKING PLACE VALUE CARDS

Place value cards can be used to show a number.

These place value cards show
8 thousands 5 hundreds 2 tens
and 8 ones.
They show the number 8528.

Make a set of place value cards.
A good size is 4cm by 3cm.
Make 10 cards for the numbers 0 to 9.
Make 10 cards for 00, 10, 20, 30, 40, 50, 60, 70, 80, 90.
Make 10 cards to show the hundreds.
Make 10 cards to show the thousands.

Ask your partner to write down a number. Make this number
using place value cards.

GAMES 1:6

FAST CARD — a game for a group.

You will need: one pack of place value cards for each player.

Choose a leader.
The leader calls out a number.
Each person in the group makes this number using place value cards.
The last person to finish is out.
Do this again until only one person is left.
This person is the new leader.

FIRST TO 20 — a game for a group.

You will need: 4 packs of place value cards.

Mix the cards up.
Choose a leader.
Give 10 cards to each player. Put the rest in a pile.
The leader calls out a number.
If you are able to make that number with your cards you get 5 points.
The winner is the first person to get 20 points.
This person is the new leader.
After each turn you *may* swap 2 of your cards for 2 from the pile.

PUTTING WHOLE NUMBERS IN ORDER

DISCUSSION 1:7

- The big cat shown can run at 112 km/h. A deer can run at 95km/h. A bird can dive through the air at 137km/h. Which of these can move the fastest? Which is the next fastest? **Discuss**.

In 1969 the first man walked on the moon. In 1978 the first test-tube baby was born in England. Which of these took place first? **Discuss**.

- Mary, Amanda and Kieran were asked to put these numbers in order from largest to smallest.

  852,   89,   86,   962

Mary said, "We must look at the hundreds place first. 962 must come first because it has the biggest digit in the hundreds place."

Amanda said, "Well 852 must come second because it is the only other number with a digit in the hundreds place."

continued . . .

...from previous page

Kieran asked, "Why do we look at the hundreds place first?"

What might the others have said? **Discuss.**

Mary went on, "The other 2 numbers both have 8 in the tens place, so how are we going to tell which is the bigger?"

What might the others say? **Discuss.**

Discuss how Mary, Amanda and Kieran might put these numbers in order.

1182,   1282,   1228,   1193,   1225

Worked Example   Five students were in a cooking contest. Marks were given out of 200. The results were:

(a) Who came first?

(b) Who came third?

(c) Who got the lowest mark?

Results	
Hannah	157
Sarah	184
Cameron	170
Arthur	185
Amelia	173

Answer   We must put the numbers in order from largest to smallest. We get 185, 184, 173, 170, 157.

(a) Arthur came first as his mark is highest.

(b) Amelia came third as her mark is the third highest.

(c) Hannah got the lowest mark.

EXERCISE 1:8

1. A competition was held to see who could get the most sponsors in a spellathon.

    The 5 best are shown on the chart.

NAME	NUMBER OF SPONSORS
JANE	23
ALEX	19
MICHAEL	29
ALISON	33
LIZ	27

    (a) Who got the most sponsors?

    (b) Who got the least number of sponsors?

    (c) Who got the third highest number of sponsors?

2.

Six people were asked how tall they were. They were 148cm, 142cm, 151cm, 143cm, 139cm and 149cm. Put these in order from tallest to shortest.

3. The Topp Family were planning a holiday.
   Belinda wrote down how much it cost to fly to some places.

Crete   £1345
Athens   £1390
Austria   £950
Riviera   £1175

Write the list in order. Put the one that costs the most first.

4. Put these numbers in order from biggest to smallest.

   (a) 486, 397, 453, 468   (b) 1279, 1297, 1379, 1973

5. Write these numbers in order from smallest to biggest.

   (a) 504, 540, 444, 450   (b) 1397, 1973, 1937, 1097

Review   The books on a shelf in the library had got out of order. Kapil was asked to sort them. The numbers are written on the books.

What order would Kapil put the books in?

GAME 1:9

REMEMBER — a game for a group

● **You will need:** one set of place value cards.

Turn all of the place value cards face down on the floor.
Mix them up.
Take turns to pick up 4 cards.
Make the biggest number you can, using the cards.

Note: If you pick up

| 6000 | 80 | 40 | 2 |

then you can only use one of the tens cards. The biggest
number you could make is 6082.

Write down the number you made. Put the cards back on the
floor, face down.

The person who has made the biggest number after everyone
has had 5 turns is the winner.

● **You will need:** 2 sets of place value cards.

Play the same game.

GREATER THAN and LESS THAN

384 is greater than 296   427 is less than 449

Instead of writing this in words we can use > and <

> means "is greater than"   < means "is less than"

We can write   384 > 296 and 427 < 449.

Worked Example   Which of < or > goes between the two numbers?

(a) 531   896   (b) 491   479

Answer   (a) 531 is less than 896 so we write   531 < 896.

(b) 491 is greater than 479 so we write   491 > 479.

EXERCISE 1:10

Copy the box below.
Work out which of < or > goes between the numbers on the left. Draw a
line from the two numbers to > or <. The first one is done for you.
486 is greater than 342. A line is drawn to >.

How many lines cross the red rectangle?

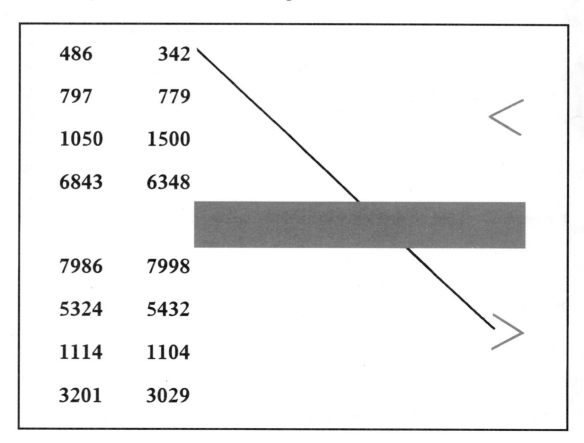

INVESTIGATION 1:11

DICE NUMBERS

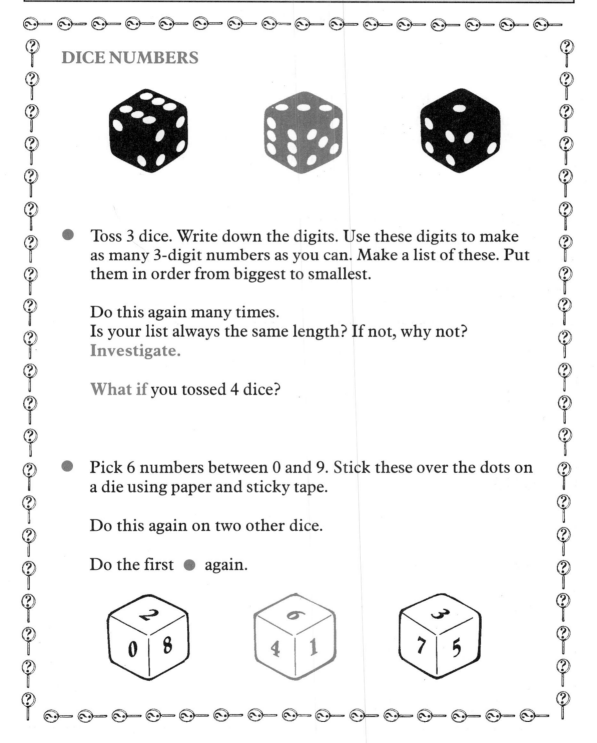

- Toss 3 dice. Write down the digits. Use these digits to make as many 3-digit numbers as you can. Make a list of these. Put them in order from biggest to smallest.

  Do this again many times.
  Is your list always the same length? If not, why not?
  Investigate.

  What if you tossed 4 dice?

- Pick 6 numbers between 0 and 9. Stick these over the dots on a die using paper and sticky tape.

  Do this again on two other dice.

  Do the first ● again.

WORK THIS OUT

Find the smallest number with 4 digits in which

- the number of hundreds minus the number of tens equals the number of thousands

- the number of tens minus the number of thousands equals the number of ones

- the number of ones is 2 more than the number of thousands

Games

GAME and DISCUSSION 2:1

● MAKE TEN — a game for 2 players

You will need: 3 blue counters
3 red counters
the board below

Decide who starts.
Player 1 puts a counter on a number.
Player 2 puts a counter on a number.
Players take turns to put a counter on a number or move one of their counters to another number.
You may not move to a number that already has a counter on it.
The winner is the first person to make 10 with 3 counters.

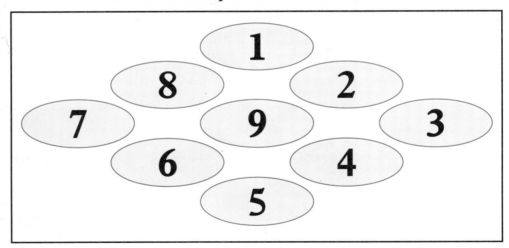

● What other games do you know? Do you have to add, subtract, multiply or divide in them? Think of sports games, board games, card games, funfair games, video games . . . Discuss.

● Make up a game of your own. Make sure the players have to add or subtract in your game. Discuss.

ADDITION and SUBTRACTION

It is best to add and subtract numbers up to 20 in your head. The addition facts on this table should be learnt.

+	0	1	2	3	4	5	6	7	8	9	10	11	12	13	14	15	16	17	18	19	20
0	0	1	2	3	4	5	6	7	8	9	10	11	12	13	14	15	16	17	18	19	20
1	1	2	3	4	5	6	7	8	9	10	11	12	13	14	15	16	17	18	19	20	
2	2	3	4	5	6	7	8	9	10	11	12	13	14	15	16	17	18	19	20		
3	3	4	5	6	7	8	9	10	11	12	13	14	15	16	17	18	19	20			
4	4	5	6	7	8	9	10	11	12	13	14	15	16	17	18	19	20				
5	5	6	7	8	9	10	11	12	13	14	15	16	17	18	19	20					
6	6	7	8	9	10	11	12	13	14	15	16	17	18	19	20						
7	7	8	9	10	11	12	13	14	15	16	17	18	19	20							
8	8	9	10	11	12	13	14	15	16	17	18	19	20								
9	9	10	11	12	13	14	15	16	17	18	19	20									
10	10	11	12	13	14	15	16	17	18	19	20										

DISCUSSION 2:2

- How can you use the addition table to work out subtractions? **Discuss.**

- 4 + 7 = 11

  Anna said, "The total of 4 and 7 is 11". Think of other ways you could say this. **Discuss.** You might use some of these words

  ADD
  PLUS
  TOGETHER
  SUM

continued . . .

- 13 − 5 = 8

  Tony said, "The difference between 13 and 5 is 8". Find other ways of saying this. **Discuss.** Use words such as

  MINUS
  SUBTRACT
  TAKE AWAY
  LESS

INVESTIGATION 2:3

ORDER

"It doesn't matter what order you add numbers in."

Investigate to see if this is true. Try out lots of examples.

What if the word subtract was used instead of add?
Investigate.

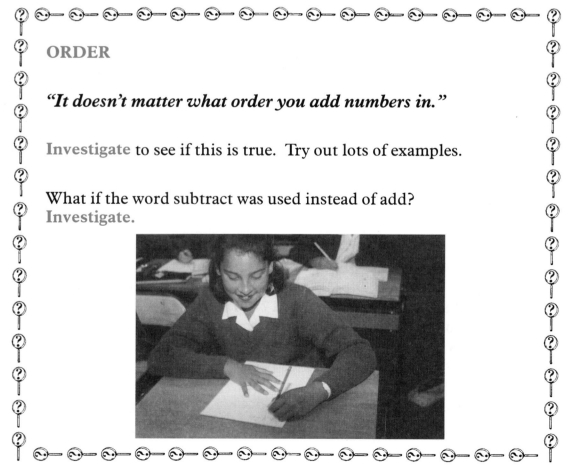

PRACTICAL and DISCUSSION 2:4

Work in Pairs

4 + 3	2 + 7	5 + 4
12 + 5	9 + 3	11 + 6
0 + 11	16 − 0	20 + 0
6 + 11	12 + 8	9 + 11
13 − 7	16 − 7	18 − 7
9 − 9	12 − 12	15 − 15
6 + 8	9 + 6	8 + 9
15 + 4	16 + 3	13 + 7
11 − 3	13 − 4	15 − 8
17 − 7	18 − 8	19 − 9
12 − 6	14 − 8	16 − 5

Write down the answers to the first box. Ask your partner to time how long it takes. Do this again for the second and third boxes. Did you get faster?

Write out each addition or subtraction above on a small card or piece of paper. Put these in a pile face down. Work with your partner. One person picks up the cards one by one and gives the answer. Is the answer right or wrong? The right answers are put in one pile and the wrong answers in another. **Discuss** how you could make this into a game.

- **Discuss** other ways you could practise your addition and subtraction facts. Choose one way to practise with.

EXERCISE 2:5

1. Find the answer to

    (a) $5 + 9$ (b) $6 + 0$ (c) $11 - 7$ (d) $15 + 3$ (e) $12 + 6$

    (f) $9 - 4$ (g) $8 + 5$ (h) $10 - 6$ (i) $8 + 7$ (j) $11 - 3$

    (k) $12 + 3$ (l) $13 - 4$ (m) $13 + 5$ (n) $16 + 4$ (o) $9 + 8$

    (p) $\begin{array}{r} 4 \\ + 15 \\ \hline \end{array}$ (q) $\begin{array}{r} 9 \\ - 6 \\ \hline \end{array}$ (r) $\begin{array}{r} 14 \\ - 3 \\ \hline \end{array}$ (s) $\begin{array}{r} 11 \\ + 0 \\ \hline \end{array}$ (t) $\begin{array}{r} 18 \\ - 11 \\ \hline \end{array}$

2. What is the missing number?

    (a) $4 + \square = 12$ (b) $11 + \square = 15$ (c) $11 - 6 = \square$

    (d) $12 - 7 = \square$ (e) $9 - \square = 1$ (f) $8 + \square = 8$

    (g) $19 - 7 = \square$ (h) $\square - 4 = 4$ (i) $9 + \square = 18$

    (j) $20 - 8 = \square$ (k) $14 + \square = 20$ (l) $11 + \square = 11$

    (m) $0 + \square = 0$ (n) $14 - \square = 7$ (o) $\square - 7 = 5$

3. Allan and Marlene had saved their
    pocket money.

    Allan had £12 and Marlene had £5.
    They wanted to buy their mother a set
    of coffee mugs for £19.
    Did they have enough money?

4. Angela is 15. Lance is 11. What is the difference in their ages?

5. Anjali took 9 minutes to walk to the bus stop. She waited for the bus for 7 minutes. How long was this altogether?

6. There were 19 people on a train. After it stopped at a station, 7 were left. How many got off?

7. □ + △ = 15. What numbers could △ and □ be? Write down as many as you can.

8. Astrid said, "I have 20p in my pocket." What coins might Astrid have in her pocket? Find as many different answers as you can.

9. Find ways of finishing these addition squares. Is there more than one way?

(a)
+	5	
8		
		16

(b)
+	4	
9		16

(c)
+		
	12	15
	7	

Review 1   Find the answer to

     (a) 16 – 4   (b) 8 + 6   (c) 12 – 4   (d) 17 – 11

Review 2   Rachel got 8 marks for part one of her test and 9 marks for the second part. What was her total mark?

Review 3   Hugh's sister lost £5. She had £17 to start with. How much money did she have left?

PUZZLES 2:6

1. MAGIC DIAMONDS

Copy these magic diamonds. Each row of 3 circles joined
by lines must add up to the same number. Fill in the other circles.

(a)

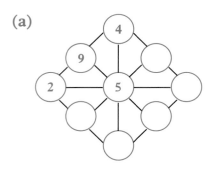

(b)

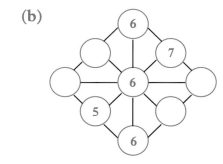

2. MAGIC CIRCLE

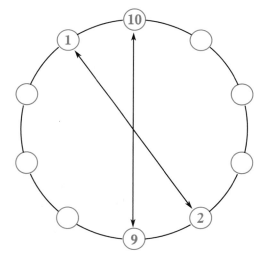

Trace this circle. The numbers 1 to 10 are to be put in the
circles. When you add any two numbers next to each other,
they must add to the same total as the two numbers opposite
them. For instance, 1 and 10 add to the same as 9 and 2. Fill in
the rest of the circles. Is there more than one way of filling this
in?

GAME 2:7

LESS THAN 20 — a game for a group

First. On a piece of card, draw 9 squares. Put one number between 0 and 20 in each square.

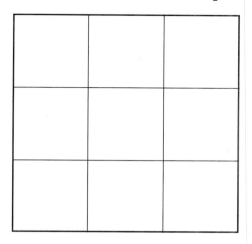

You will need: a card for each person
counters

To Play

Choose a leader.

The leader calls out an addition or subtraction which has answer of 20 or less. For instance 19 – 14 or 8 + 3.

If the answer is a number on your card, cover the number with a counter.

The winner is the first person to have all of his or her numbers covered.

This person is the new leader.

INVESTIGATION 2:8

SQUARES WITHIN SQUARES

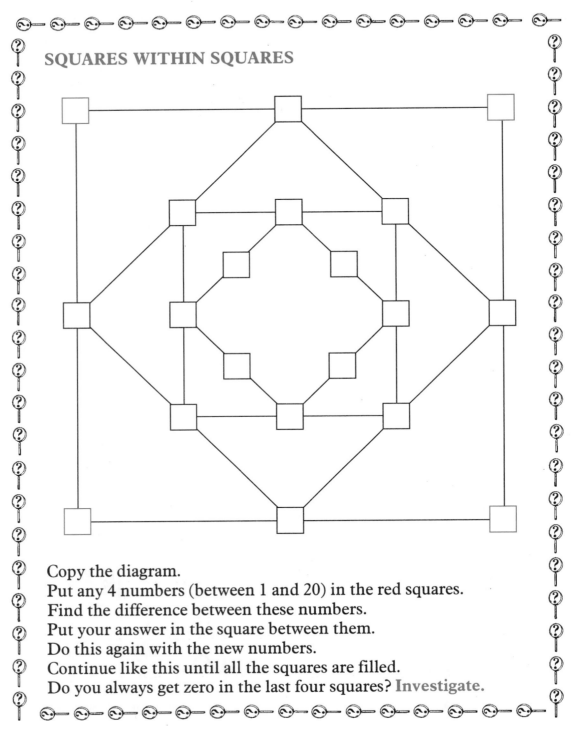

Copy the diagram.

Put any 4 numbers (between 1 and 20) in the red squares.

Find the difference between these numbers.

Put your answer in the square between them.

Do this again with the new numbers.

Continue like this until all the squares are filled.

Do you always get zero in the last four squares? Investigate.

DISCUSSION 2:9

● How could we add 7 + 9 using this abacus? **Discuss.**

Try lots of other additions.

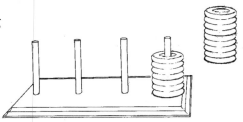

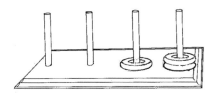

How could we use this abacus to find the answer to 12 −5? **Discuss.** Try other subtractions.

●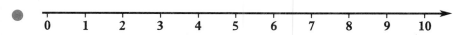

This is a number line.
What does the arrow mean? **Discuss.**
How could we use a number line to add? **Discuss.** Try lots of examples.
Make up some rules for adding on a number line. **Discuss.**

●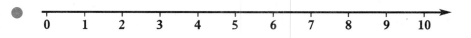

How could you use this number line to subtract? **Discuss.**
Try lots of examples.
Make up some rules for subtracting on a number line.
Discuss.

INVESTIGATION 2:10

ODDS AND EVENS

● Choose two odd numbers. Add them together. Do this again many times. What do you notice? **Investigate.**

What if you add two even numbers together?
What if you add an odd and an even number together?
Show your group what you noticed.

● $0 + 1 = 1$ $1 + 2 = 3$ $2 + 3 = 5$ $3 + 4 = 7$

What do you notice about this pattern? Can you make every odd number this way? **Investigate.**

What about even numbers? **Investigate.**

● $3 + 3 = 6$ $6 + 3 = 9$ $9 + 3 = 12$ $12 + 3 = 15$

Choose an odd number other than 1. Add it to itself. Keep adding the odd number on. Which of the numbers in the box can you make by doing this?

$$5 \qquad 8 \qquad 14$$
$$11 \quad 16 \quad 20$$

What if you began with an even number?
What if the numbers in the box were 3, 6, 7, 10, 17, 18?

MULTIPLICATION FACTS

DISCUSSION 2:11

Count the number of students. How else could you work out the number of students? **Discuss.**

Work out the total number of stars. How many lots of 2 stars are there? How could we write this using a × sign? **Discuss.**

Work out how many cherries there are using
— counting
— addition
— multiplication.

What can you say about multiplication? **Discuss.**

Multiplication is the same as adding a number again and again.
For instance 4 × 3 means 4 lots of 3 or 3 + 3 + 3 + 3.

You should learn the multiplication facts given in these two tables.

×	1	2	3	4	5
1	1	2	3	4	5
2	2	4	6	8	10
3	3	6	9	12	15
4	4	8	12	16	20
5	5	10	15	20	25

×	1	2	3	4	5	6	7	8	9	10
2	2	4	6	8	10	12	14	16	18	20
5	5	10	15	20	25	30	35	40	45	50
10	10	20	30	40	50	60	70	80	90	100

Worked Example

In a contest there were 3 heats. Each heat had 6 people. How many people took part in the contest altogether?

Answer   6 lots of 3 or 6 × 3 = 18.
18 people took part in the contest.

EXERCISE 2:12

1. Copy these tables and fill them in.

×	1	3	5
0			
2			
3			

(a)

×	2	4	10
3			
5			
10			

(b)

×	4	5	10
0			
2			
4			

(c)

2.

			T							T			
16	7	40	18	0	10	40	0	9	20	18	0	8	70

					T			
14	20	12	50	14		18	0	16	50

Copy the box. Work out each multiplication below. Put the letter beside it on the line above the answer.
The first one is done for you.

2×9 = (T) 3×3 = (C) 2×4 = (O)

5×4 = (A) 5×8 = (L) 2×5 = (P)

3×4 = (V) 2×8 = (M) 5×0 = (I)

7×10 = (N) 10×5 = (E)

2×7 = (S) 7×1 = (U)

3. Find the number in the box.

(a) $5 \times 3 = \square$ (b) $4 \times 2 = \square$ (c) $3 \times 0 = \square$

(d) $10 \times 1 = \square$ (e) $2 \times \square = 10$ (f) $3 \times 3 = \square$

(g) $\square \times 5 = 0$ (h) $\square \times 10 = 0$ (i) $3 \times \square = 12$

(j) $5 \times \square = 40$ (k) $\square \times 10 = 70$ (l) $5 \times \square = 25$

4. Joel wants to buy 5 lollies for his brothers and sisters. How much will these cost?

5. In a classroom there are 5 rows of desks. Each row has 7 desks. How many desks are there in this room?

6. T-shirts cost £5. How many could Janice buy for £35?

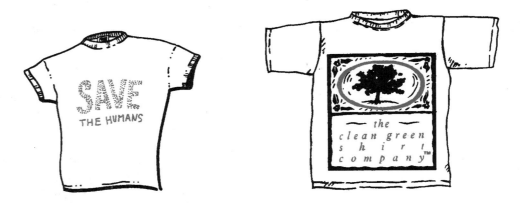

7. Murray and Asif are practising their tables. Murray told Asif his answer was 20.
   What multiplications could Murray have done to get this answer?

8. Find ways of filling in this multiplication square.

×		2	
5			5
		0	
	6		

Review 1 Find
  (a) 2 × 5   (b) 3 × 4   (c) 10 × 7   (d) 0 × 3

  (e) 5 × 8   (f) 10 × 6   (g) 5 × 9   (h) 3 × 6

  (i) 4 × 5   (j) 5 × 7

Review 2 Jake, Graham and Scott have 5 marbles each. How many marbles do they have altogether?

GAME 2:13

DICE MULTIPLICATION — a game for 2 players

You will need : 2 dice
12 different coloured counters for each player
the board shown below

Take turns to toss two dice. If you get a six you can put a counter on any number or take off one of the other players's counters. If you do not get a six, multiply the two numbers together. Put a counter on the answer. If the number has a counter on it, your turn is over.

The winner is the first person to get 3 counters in a row.
Examples of rows are   3, 4 and 5   8, 25 and 15
                      3, 9 and 3   12, 25 and 6

1	2	3	4	5
2	6	8	9	4
3	20	25	10	3
4	16	15	12	2
5	4	3	2	1

DIVISION

DISCUSSION 2:14

- Annabelle has 15 sweets. She wants to share these between 5 people. **Discuss** how to do this.

  Sharing is sometimes called dividing.
  Annabelle could have said, "15 shared between 5 gives 3".
  How can we write this using a ÷ sign? **Discuss.**
  How would Annabelle share 20 sweets? **Discuss.**

- $12 - 3 - 3 - 3 - 3 = 0$. We can take 3 away from 12, 4 times.

  How could we write this using a ÷ sign? **Discuss.**

- $3 \times \square = 12$. What number goes in the box? We can write this another way. $12 \div 3 = \square$

  How could you use the tables on **page 50** to find the answer to these? **Discuss.**

  $16 \div 4$ $20 \div 10$ $45 \div 5$ $30 \div 10$

-

  $2 + 3 + 1 + 1 = 7$

  8   **16**   **12**   **20**

  Find corner numbers for these. Does everyone in your group have the same corner numbers? **Discuss.** If each corner number must be the same, how can you find what it is for these squares? **Discuss.**

Worked Example   At a party there were 18 chocolate biscuits to be
shared between 6 people.
They all got the
same number of
biscuits. How
many did
each get?

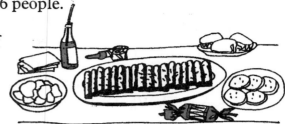

Answer   18 shared between 6 is 18 ÷ 6.
18 ÷ 6 = 3. Each person got 3 biscuits.

EXERCISE 2:15

1. Find

    (a)   10 ÷ 2   (b)   18 ÷ 3   (c)   20 ÷ 4   (d)   16 ÷ 4

    (e)   50 ÷ 10   (f)   12 ÷ 3   (g)   12 ÷ 4   (h)   25 ÷ 5

    (i)   40 ÷ 4   (j)   40 ÷ 5   (k)   40 ÷ 10   (l)   45 ÷ 5

    (m) 100 ÷ 10   (n)   70 ÷ 7   (o)   35 ÷ 5

2. Share 12 pieces of cake between 4 people so each gets the same. How
    many pieces does each get?

3. Olive and Jasmine cut a 70cm length of ribbon. They cut it into pieces
    10cm long. How many pieces did they get?

4. Sally and Mark were lost in the
    forest. They had 12 meals with them.
    They wanted these to last 6 days.
    How many meals could they have
    each day?

5. Put < or > to make these true. The first one is done for you.

    (a) $20 \div 5 > 3$ (b) $30 \div 10$ 4   (c) $18 \div 3$ 5

    (d) $60 \div 6$ 11   (e) $45 \div 9$ 3

6. $20 \div \triangle = \square$. What numbers can $\triangle$ and $\square$ be?

Review 1   Find

    (a) $14 \div 2$ (b) $80 \div 10$ (c) $12 \div 3$ (d) $30 \div 5$

    (e) $45 \div 9$ (f) $16 \div 4$ (g) $20 \div 4$

Review 2

Ruth bought tickets to a show for herself and 3 friends. It cost her £20. How much was each ticket?

DISCUSSION 2:16

● Linda said, "3 × 4 is the same as 4 × 3 so it doesn't matter what order we multiply in."

Try out lots of other examples to see if Linda is right.
Discuss.
Could Linda say something like this about division?
Discuss.

INVESTIGATION 2:17

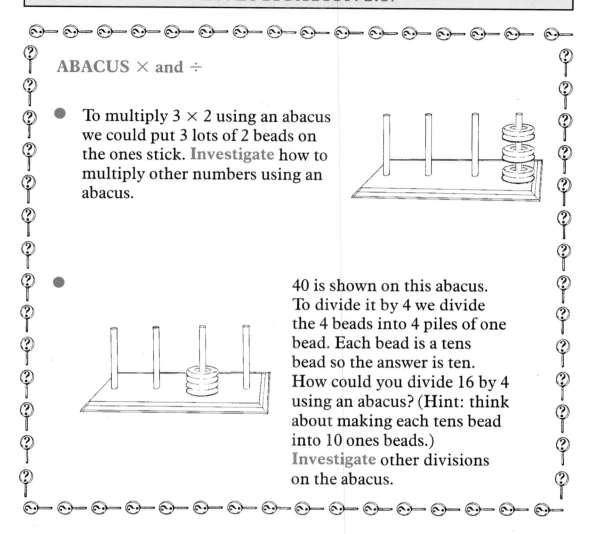

ABACUS × and ÷

● To multiply 3 × 2 using an abacus we could put 3 lots of 2 beads on the ones stick. **Investigate** how to multiply other numbers using an abacus.

● 40 is shown on this abacus. To divide it by 4 we divide the 4 beads into 4 piles of one bead. Each bead is a tens bead so the answer is ten. How could you divide 16 by 4 using an abacus? (Hint: think about making each tens bead into 10 ones beads.) **Investigate** other divisions on the abacus.

PUZZLE 2:18

WHAT NUMBER

Alana divided a number by 5.
She then added 1.
The answer was 15 less than the number she started with.
What number did she start with?

WORK THIS OUT

Put these number boxes
into 3 equal piles.
Each pile must add
to the same number.

1	2	3
3	4	5
5	6	7

Look Around You at . . .

Music

DISCUSSION 3:1

● "On the first day of Christmas
My true love sent to me
A partridge in a pear tree."

"On the second day of Christmas
My true love sent to me
Two turtle doves and a partridge in a pear tree."

How does this song carry on? What patterns can you find in this song? **Discuss.**
Think of other songs which have patterns in them. **Discuss.**

● "When we listen to music we are listening to patterns made with sound," said Tom.

Discuss what Tom said.

● Find as many patterns as you can to do with music. **Discuss.**
You could think about

— choirs
— drums
— concerts . . .

PATTERNS

PRACTICAL 3:2

With Matches — you will need about 50 matches.

2 matches

4 matches

6 matches

8 matches

3 matches

6 matches

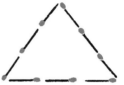

9 matches

Make the next matchstick picture for each of the patterns above. How many matches does each have?

Copy the matchstick pictures above. Write the number of matches used under each picture. Make the next picture in the pattern. How many matches did you use?

continued . . .

. . . from previous page

See if you can make;

a pattern that begins with

a pattern that begins with

Write down in your own words what patterns you have made.

Make some matchstick patterns of your own. Write about these patterns.

With Counters — you will need counters of 2 different colours.

Make this pattern with your counters. What comes next? Write about this pattern in your own words.

Make these patterns with your counters. Work out what comes next. Write about the patterns.

Make up some patterns of your own using counters. Write about them.

continued . . .

. . . from previous page

With Blocks — you will need some Multilink cubes or Lego blocks.

Make this pattern.

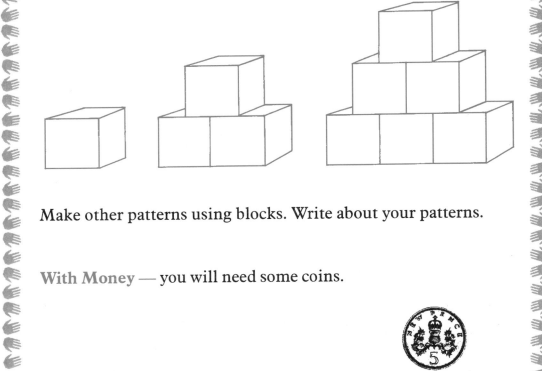

Make other patterns using blocks. Write about your patterns.

With Money — you will need some coins.

5   10   15

How else could you make the pattern 5, 10, 15 . . . using coins?
Make other patterns using coins.

NUMBER PATTERNS

DISCUSSION 3:3

● 1, 2, 1, 2, 1, 2, . . .

2, 4, 6, 8, . . .

5, 10, 15, 20, . . .

1, 2, 1, 1, 2, 2, 1, 1, 1, 2, . . .

What do you think the . . . at the end of these means?
Discuss.
Discuss how these number patterns might carry on.

●

1	2	3	4	5	6	7	8	9	10	11	12

1	2	3	4	5	6	7	8	9	10

Discuss how these number patterns might carry on.

●

C	A	T	C	A	T	C	A	T	
1	2	3	4	5	6	7	8	9	

Which letter will be above the number 12? **Discuss.**
What about the number 20?
What about the number 50?
What about the number 100? **Discuss.**

continued . . .

. . . from previous page

● Use your calculator to find how these number patterns are made. **Discuss.**

2, 4, 8, 16, 32, . . .

24, 12, 6, 3, . . .

●

What number pattern could we write for this matchstick picture?
How did you decide this? **Discuss.**

●

1p	10p	£1	£10
2p	20p	£2	£20
5p	50p	£5	£50

All of these coins and notes have been in use at some time. What patterns can you see? **Discuss.**

PRACTICAL 3:4

Use LOGO on your computer for this.

- FORWARD 120
  RIGHT 90
  FORWARD 120

  Type in these lines. What does RIGHT 90 do?

- FORWARD 60
  LEFT 90
  FORWARD 60
  RIGHT 90

  Make a pattern by typing in these lines again and again.

- FORWARD 60
  LEFT 90
  FORWARD 60
  RIGHT 90
  FORWARD 60
  RIGHT 90
  FORWARD 60
  LEFT 90

  What pattern is made by typing these lines again and again? **Investigate.**

- Make your own pattern using LOGO.

EXERCISE 3:5

1. Find the missing number.

    (a) 2, 4, □, 8, 10   (b) 3, 6, 9, □, 15   (c) 5, □, 15, 20

    (d) 4, 8, 16, □, 64   (e) 40, 20, □, 5   (f) 1, 2, 4, 7, □, 16

2. Copy these patterns. Show what comes next.

    (a) ● ● ● ● ● ●   (b) ● ● ● ● ● ● ● ● ● ● ●

    (c) ● ● ● ● ● ● ● ● ● ● ●

3. Write down a number pattern for these.

    (a)

    (b)

4. What is the next number in these number patterns?

    (a) 10, 20, 30, 40, . . .   (b) 25, 20, 15, 10, . . .

    (c) 1, 1, 2, 2, 1, 1, 3, 3, 1, 1, . . .   (d) 2, 6, 10, 14, . . .

    (e) 1, 9, 17, 25, . . .   (f) 2, 4, 8, 16, . . .

    (g) 3, 5, 8, 12, 17, . . .   (h) 1, 3, 6, 10, . . .

    (i) 6, 9, 8, 11, 10, 13, 12, . . .

5. If this pattern carries on, what will be above 27?

Review 1 Write down a number pattern for this matchstick picture.

Review 2 What is the next number?

(a) 15, 20, 25, 30, . . .   (b) 1, 2, 4, 8, . . .   (c) 6, 12, 18, . . .

(d) 2, 6, 18, . . .   (e) 64, 32, 16, . . .   (f) 20, 1, 19, 2, 18, 3, . . .

PRACTICAL 3:6

Use **LOGO** on your computer. Type in these lines.

```
FORWARD  40
RIGHT  90
FORWARD  60
RIGHT  90
FORWARD  80
RIGHT  90
FORWARD  100
RIGHT  90
```

What pattern do you notice? How could you carry this pattern on? **Investigate.**

u twat!   QP

INVESTIGATION 3:7

ROUND AND ROUND

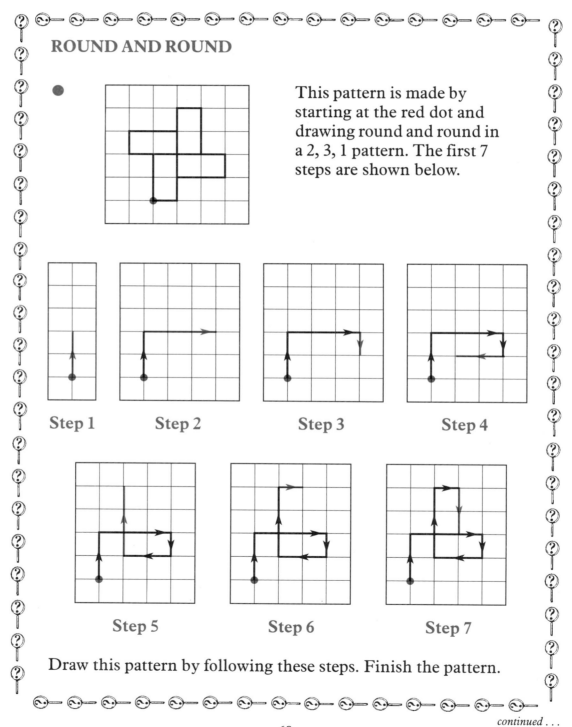

This pattern is made by starting at the red dot and drawing round and round in a 2, 3, 1 pattern. The first 7 steps are shown below.

Step 1   Step 2   Step 3   Step 4

Step 5   Step 6   Step 7

Draw this pattern by following these steps. Finish the pattern.

continued . . .

. . . from previous page

What if you drew round and round in a 3, 2, 4 pattern?
What if you drew round and round in these patterns?

1, 2, 3
3, 6, 2
3, 2, 5
6, 1, 5
3, 4, 1, 2
4, 5, 1, 3, 1

Investigate many round and round patterns.

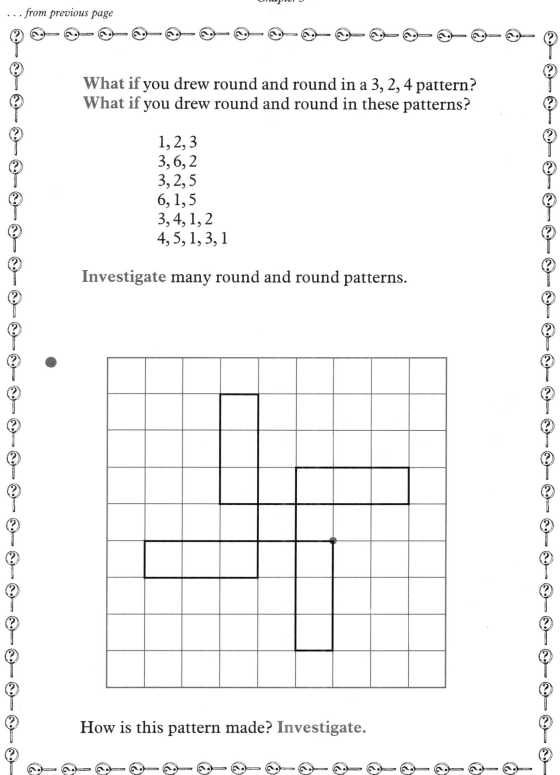

How is this pattern made? **Investigate.**

GAME 3:8

FROGS — a game for groups of 4

You will need: 5 sheets of paper

The Game

There are 4 frogs in the lily pond. They begin on the leaves as shown.

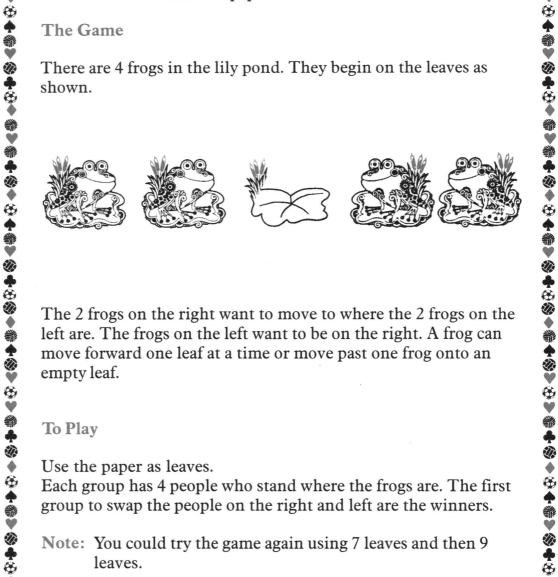

The 2 frogs on the right want to move to where the 2 frogs on the left are. The frogs on the left want to be on the right. A frog can move forward one leaf at a time or move past one frog onto an empty leaf.

To Play

Use the paper as leaves.
Each group has 4 people who stand where the frogs are. The first group to swap the people on the right and left are the winners.

Note: You could try the game again using 7 leaves and then 9 leaves.

PUZZLE 3:9

SHAPE UP and DOWN

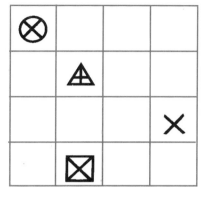

Put these shapes
into the boxes so
that each row and
column has only
one of each shape.

ADDITION and SUBTRACTION PATTERNS

DISCUSSION 3:10

● Deborah was asked to add 23 + 9. She said, "First I add 10
and then I take 1 away. So I say 23 + 10 = 33, take away 1 is
32."

Discuss Deborah's way of adding 9 to 23.
"What about when you have to subtract 9?" asked Shane.

What do you think Deborah said now? **Discuss.**

Discuss quick ways of adding and subtracting 8. What
about 7, 6, 5, 4 and 3? **Discuss.**

continued . . .

. . . from previous page

●   7 + 10 = 17   5 + 9 = 14
       17 + 10 = 27   15 + 9 = 24
       27 + 10 = 37   25 + 9 = 34
       37 + 10 = 47   35 + 9 = 44

What would the next 3 lines of each of these be? **Discuss.**
Make up 5 more number patterns like these. Give them to
someone else in your group. Ask them to write down the
next 3 lines of each. What do you notice about these
patterns? **Discuss.**

●   27 = 20 + 7   34 = 30 + 4

Write the numbers in the box in the same way 27 and 34
have been written.

51	46	18	63	19	82

How could you add 27 and 34 by writing them this way?
Discuss.
Add some of the numbers in the box together. **Discuss** how
you did it.

Worked Example   Copy and fill in the gaps.

$$39 + 53 = 30 + \_\_\_\_ + \_\_\_\_ + 3$$
$$= \_\_\_\_ + 50 + \_\_\_\_ + \_\_\_\_$$
$$= \_\_\_\_ + \_\_\_\_$$
$$= \_\_\_\_ + \_\_\_\_ + \_\_\_\_$$
$$= \_\_\_\_ + \_\_\_\_$$
$$= \_\_\_\_$$

Answer $39 + 53 = 30 + 9 + 50 + 3$
$$= 30 + 50 + 9 + 3$$
$$= 80 + 12$$
$$= 80 + 10 + 2$$
$$= 90 + 2$$
$$= 92$$

EXERCISE 3:11

1. Copy these and fill in the boxes.

    (a) $14 + 9 = 14 + 10 - \square$
         $\quad\quad = \square$

    (b) $35 + 8 = 35 + 10 - \square$
         $\quad\quad = \square$

    (c) $26 - 9 = 26 - 10 + \square$
         $\quad\quad = \square$

    (d) $74 - 8 = 74 - \square + \square$
         $\quad\quad = \square$

    (e) $47 + 9 = \square$

    (f) $24 - 8 = \square$

    (g) $83 + 8 = \square$

    (h) $51 - 9 = \square$

2. Write the next 3 lines for each.

    (a) $7 + 8 = 15$ (b) $1 + 5 = 6$ (c) $9 + 7 = 16$ (d) $5 + 3 = 8$
        $17 + 8 = 25$ $1 + 6 = 7$ $19 + 7 = 26$ $6 + 3 = 9$
        $27 + 8 = 35$ $1 + 7 = 8$ $29 + 7 = 36$ $7 + 3 = 10$

3. Write about the patterns in **question 2** in your own words.

4. Find as many ways as you can of filling the gaps with 2, 3, 4, 5, 6 or 7.
    Do not use a number more than once in each question.

    (a) ____ $+$ ____ $= 7$ (b) ____ $+$ ____ $+$ ____ $= 9$

    (c) ____ $+$ ____ $+$ ____ $= 10$ (d) ____ $+$ ____ $-$ ____ $= 9$

    (e) ____ $+$ ____ $-$ ____ $= 4$ (f) ____ $+$ ____ $-$ ____ $= 6$

    (g) ____ $-$ ____ $-$ ____ $= 1$ (h) ____ $-$ ____ $-$ ____ $= 0$

5. Copy and fill in the gaps.

(a) $16 + 23 = 10 + 6 + 20 + 3$
              $= 10 +$ ____ $+ 6 + 3$
              $=$ ____ $+ 9$
              $=$ ____

(b) $24 + 35 = 20 + 4 + 30 +$ ____
              $= 20 +$ ____ $+$ ____ $+$ ____
              $= 50 +$ ____
              $=$ ____

(c) $37 + 24 = 30 +$ ____ $+ 20 +$ ____

$= 30 +$ ____ $+$ ____ $+$ ____

$=$ ____ $+ 11$

$=$ ____ $+$ ____ $+$ ____

$=$ ____ $+$ ____

$=$ ____

(d) $26 + 57 =$ ____ $+$ ____ $+$ ____ $+ 7$

$=$ ____ $+ 50 +$ ____ $+$ ____

$=$ ____ $+$ ____

$=$ ____ $+$ ____ $+$ ____

$=$ ____ $+$ ____

$=$ ____

6.

$$\Delta + \square = 15$$

Find as many numbers as you can for Δ and $\square$.

Review 1 Copy and fill in the boxes.

(a) $27 + 9 = 27 + \square - 1$

$= \square$

(b) $83 - 8 = 83 - \square + \square$

$= \square$

Review 2 Copy and fill in the gaps with one of 2, 3, 4, 5, 6 or 7. Use each number only once in each question.

(a) ____ $+$ ____ $+$ ____ $= 12$

(b) ____ $+$ ____ $-$ ____ $= 2$

Review 3 Copy and fill in the gaps.

$29 + 42 = 20 +$ ____ $+ 40 +$ ____

$= 20 +$ ____ $+ 9 +$ ____

$= 60 +$ ____

$= 60 +$ ____ $+$ ____

$=$ ____ $+$ ____

$=$ ____

DISCUSSION 3:12

● $1 + 2 = 3$
$4 + 5 + 6 = 7 + 8$
$9 + 10 + 11 + 12 = 13 + 14 + 15$

What do you think the next 3 lines will be? **Discuss.**

INVESTIGATION 3:13

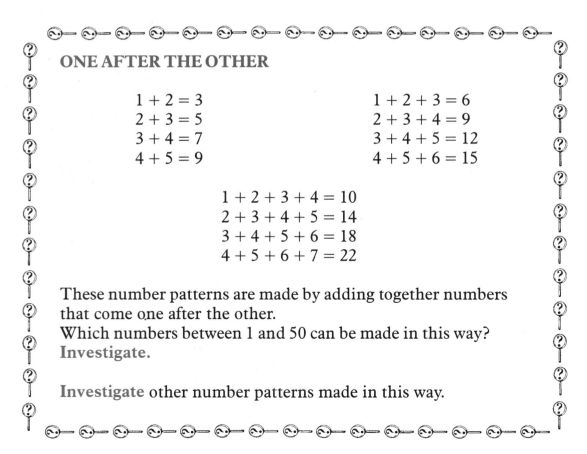

ONE AFTER THE OTHER

$1 + 2 = 3$ $1 + 2 + 3 = 6$
$2 + 3 = 5$ $2 + 3 + 4 = 9$
$3 + 4 = 7$ $3 + 4 + 5 = 12$
$4 + 5 = 9$ $4 + 5 + 6 = 15$

$1 + 2 + 3 + 4 = 10$
$2 + 3 + 4 + 5 = 14$
$3 + 4 + 5 + 6 = 18$
$4 + 5 + 6 + 7 = 22$

These number patterns are made by adding together numbers that come one after the other.
Which numbers between 1 and 50 can be made in this way?
Investigate.

Investigate other number patterns made in this way.

MULTIPLICATION PATTERNS

DISCUSSION 3:14

- Sam was asked to multiply 4×8 in his head.
  "I don't know my four times facts", said Sam.

  How could Sam use $2 \times 8 = 16$ to work out the answer to 4×8?

$2 \times 1 = 2$	$2 \times 2 = 4$	$2 \times 3 = 6$	$2 \times 4 = 8$
$4 \times 1 = 4$	$4 \times 2 = 8$	$4 \times 3 = 12$	$4 \times 4 = 16$

  What would the next 3 pairs of this pattern be?
  Discuss.

$3 \times 1 = 3$	$3 \times 2 = 6$
$6 \times 1 = 6$	$6 \times 2 = 12$

  What would the next 3 pairs of this pattern be?
  Discuss.

- When Dean was asked to multiply 15×9 he wrote this.
  Discuss Dean's way.

$$15 \times 9 = 10 \times 9 + 5 \times 9$$
$$= 90 + 45$$
$$= 90 + 40 + 5$$
$$= 130 + 5$$
$$= 135$$

INVESTIGATION 3:15

MULTIPLICATION FACTS SQUARE

×	1	2	3	4	5	6	7	8	9	10
1	1	2	3	4	5	6	7	8	9	10
2	2	4	6	8	10	12	14	16	18	20
3	3	6	9	12	15	18	21	24	27	30
4	4	8	12	16	20	24	28	32	36	40
5	5	10	15	20	25	30	35	40	45	50
6	6	12	18	24	30	36	42	48	54	60
7	7	14	21	28	35	42	49	56	63	70
8	8	16	24	32	40	48	56	64	72	80
9	9	18	27	36	45	54	63	72	81	90
10	10	20	30	40	50	60	70	80	90	100

What do you notice about the 3 times facts and the 6 times facts?

Make some copies of this table.
Investigate to find other multiplication facts patterns.

EXERCISE 3:16

1. Write down the next 3 lines for each.

    (a) $4 \times 2 = 8$
        $4 \times 3 = 12$
        $4 \times 4 = 16$

    (b) $6 \times 1 = 6$
        $6 \times 2 = 12$
        $6 \times 3 = 18$

    (c) $5 \times 5 = 25$
        $5 \times 6 = 30$
        $5 \times 7 = 35$

(d) $9 \times 2 = 18$
$9 \times 3 = 27$
$9 \times 4 = 36$

(e) $8 \times 5 = 40$
$8 \times 6 = 48$
$8 \times 7 = 56$

(f) $1 \times 1 = 1$
$2 \times 2 = 4$
$3 \times 3 = 9$

2. Write about the patterns in **question 1** in your own words.

3. Copy and fill in the gaps.

(a) $18 \times 5 = 10 \times 5 + 8 \times 5$
$= \_\_\_\_ + 40$
$= \_\_\_\_$

(b) $15 \times 7 = 10 \times 7 + \_\_\_\_ \times 7$
$= 70 + \_\_\_\_$
$= 70 + 30 + \_\_\_\_$
$= \_\_\_\_ + \_\_\_\_$
$= \_\_\_\_$

(c) $17 \times 4 = 10 \times 4 + \_\_\_\_ \times \_\_\_\_$
$= 40 + \_\_\_\_$
$= 40 + \_\_\_\_ + \_\_\_\_$
$= \_\_\_\_ + \_\_\_\_$
$= \_\_\_\_$

(d) $14 \times 3 = 10 \times \_\_\_\_ + \_\_\_\_ \times \_\_\_\_$
$= \_\_\_\_ + \_\_\_\_$
$= \_\_\_\_ + \_\_\_\_ + \_\_\_\_$
$= \_\_\_\_ + \_\_\_\_$
$= \_\_\_\_$

4. Work these out without the calculator.

(a) 4×8 (b) 6×5 (c) 4×7 (d) 9×3

(e) 4×6 (f) 6×3 (g) 9×4

5.

Find as many numbers as you can for ● and ★.

Review 1   Write down the next 3 lines for each.

(a) $7 \times 1 = 7$
$7 \times 2 = 14$
$7 \times 3 = 21$

(b) $8 \times 3 = 24$
$8 \times 4 = 32$
$8 \times 5 = 40$

Review 2   Copy and fill in the gaps.

(a) $16 \times 5 = 10 \times$ ____ $+ 6 \times$ ____
$= 50 +$ ____
$=$ ____

(b) $13 \times 6 = 10 \times$ ____ $+$ ____ $\times 6$
$=$ ____ $+$ ____
$=$ ____ $+$ ____ $+$ ____
$=$ ____ $+$ ____
$=$ ____

Review 3   Work these out without the calculator.

(a) 6×8 (b) 8×3 (c) 9×5

DISCUSSION 3:17

●
$$1 \times 9 = 10 - 1$$
$$2 \times 9 = 20 - 2$$
$$3 \times 9 = 30 - 3$$

Discuss this number pattern. Write down the next 3 lines.
How would you fill in $9 \times 9 = \square - \square$?
Can you write a pattern like this starting $1 \times 8 = 10 - 2$?

●
$$3 \times 3 = 2 \times 2 + 2 + 3$$
$$4 \times 4 = 3 \times 3 + 3 + 4$$
$$5 \times 5 = 4 \times 4 + 4 + 5$$

Discuss this number pattern. Write down the next 2 lines.

continued . . .

. . . from previous page

●
$$3 \times 3 = 4 \times 2 + 1$$
$$4 \times 4 = 5 \times 3 + 1$$
$$5 \times 5 = 6 \times 4 + 1$$

Write down the next 3 lines of this number pattern. **Discuss.**

Try and make up some more patterns which begin
$$3 \times 3 =$$
$$4 \times 4 =$$
$$5 \times 5 =$$

INVESTIGATION 3:18

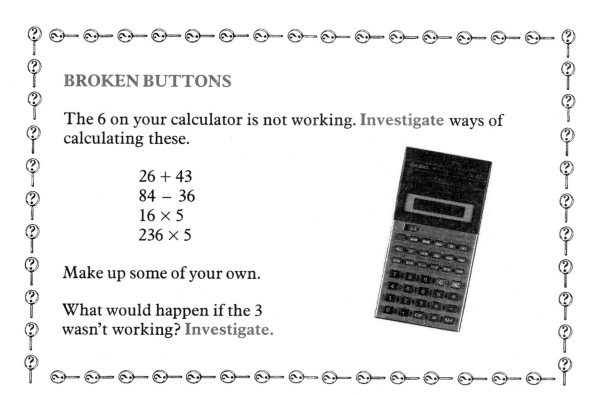

BROKEN BUTTONS

The 6 on your calculator is not working. **Investigate** ways of calculating these.

$$26 + 43$$
$$84 - 36$$
$$16 \times 5$$
$$236 \times 5$$

Make up some of your own.

What would happen if the 3 wasn't working? **Investigate.**

DIVIDING BY 2, 5 and 10

We say one number is divisible by another if there is no remainder. So 8 is divisible by 2. 7 is not divisible by 2.

INVESTIGATION AND DISCUSSION 3:19

- $52 \div 5$ gives | 10.4 |

  $65 \div 5$ gives | $13.$ |

  Which of 52 or 65 is able to be divided by 5 so there is no remainder? How do you know this? Discuss.

  Divide these numbers by 5.

  | 73   96   85   67   90   45

  Which are divisible by 5? Discuss.

  Choose some 3-digit numbers. Divide them by 5.
  What do you notice about the numbers which are divisible by 5? Investigate.

  Can you tell which of these will be divisible by 5?

  | 1837   4320   8645   2783

- Choose some 2 and 3-digit numbers. Investigate to find which ones are divisible by 10. Investigate to find which ones are divisible by 2.
  Finish these sentences. Discuss.

  All numbers that are divisible by 5 _____.
  All numbers that are divisible by 10 _____.
  All numbers that are divisible by 2 _____.

INVESTIGATION 3:20

DIVIDING

Sara wrote on the board, "All numbers that are divisible by 10 are also divisible by 2 and 5."

Investigate to see if this is true by trying out lots of examples.

"Does that mean if a number if divisible by 2 and 5 it will also be divisible by 10?" asked Alice.

Investigate to find the answer to Alice's question.

A number is **divisible by 2** if it is an even number.

A number is **divisible by 5** if it ends in 0 or 5.

A number is **divisible by 10** if it ends in 0.

EXERCISE 3:21

1. Copy the box.
   Colour all the numbers which are divisible by 5. What pattern does this make?

82	53	96	25	112	107	54
217	196	99	50	31	382	851
1050	105	100	95	130	275	860
67	102	91	60	1111	398	147
1872	3	4	425	78	79	104

2. Make another copy of the box in **question 1**. Colour all the numbers that are divisible by 2. What pattern does this make?

3. Which number doesn't belong in the list? Why?

   (a) 5, 70, 85, 155, 2185, 63, 20

   (b) 50, 110, 5060, 75, 90, 480

   (c) 12, 26, 40, 1140, 1255, 810

4. Here are 2 groups of numbers. Which group would you put 175 in? Why?

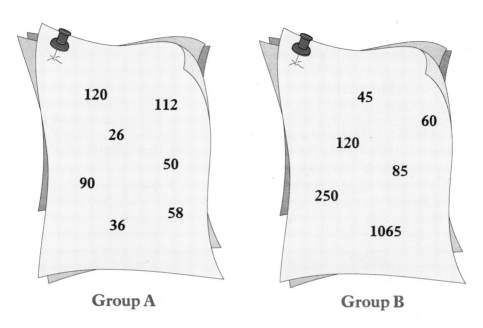

Group A · Group B

Review

| 87 | 50 | 115 | 960 | 435 | 114 |

Write down all the numbers in the box which are

(a) divisible by 5

(b) divisible by 2

(c) divisible by 10

(d) divisible by 2 and 5.

(e) Why are the answers to (c) and (d) the same?

GAME 3:22

BUZZ — a game for a class.

Sit or stand in a circle.
Choose someone to start.
This person says 1, the next person says 2, the next 3 and so on.
When a number that is divisible by 5 is to be said, the person must say "Buzz" instead of the number.
If this person says the number, he or she is out.
The winner is the last person left.

You could play the game again for numbers divisible by 10 or 2.

WORK THIS OUT

1. Dougal's age is divisible by 5 but not 10.
   Tina's age is divisible by 2 but not 5.
   Dougal is 3 years older than Tina.
   Both are younger than 30. How old are Dougal and Tina"? Is there more than one answer?

2. A class was asked to get into twos. There was 1 person left over. The same class got into threes. There was 1 person left over again. When the same class got into fives, no one was left over. How many were in this class if there were fewer than 40?

More Working with Numbers

The Shop

PRACTICAL AND DISCUSSION 4:1

Go to one of your local shops. Find as many different numbers as you can. Write these down.

When is addition and subtraction used at this shop? **Discuss.**

When is multiplication and division used at this shop? **Discuss.**

Work in groups to make a poster, display or tape or give a talk to show how the shop works with numbers.

HARDER ADDITION and SUBTRACTION

DISCUSSION 4:2

● Jasmine wanted to add her scores for the first 7 holes of mini-golf. She wrote

$2 + 5 + 8 + 4 + 3 + 9 + 6 = 37$

Her brother James checked her answer by writing the numbers down the page.

$$
\begin{array}{r}
2 \\
5 \\
8 \\
4 \\
3 \\
9 \\
+\ 6 \\
\hline
37
\end{array}
$$

Discuss which way is best.

Jasmine's father added his scores by finding groups of numbers that added to 10 or 20. **Discuss.**

$8 + 4 + 7 + 5 + 2 + 6 + 6$

$$
\begin{array}{r}
5 + 7 + 8 = 20 \\
6 + 4 = 10 \\
2 + 6 = \underline{\ 8\ } + \\
38
\end{array}
$$

● $9 + 2 - 3 + 4 - 5 =$

*When we have addition **and** subtraction we must **always** work from the left to the right.*
Is this true? **Discuss.**

Work out the answers to these. **Discuss.**

$11 - 3 + 4 - 2 - 1 =$
$8 + 9 - 5 - 6 + 4 =$

PUZZLE 4:3

MAKE a NUMBER

```
8  5  7  6  5  5  6  6  4  3  9  2  7  4  7
6  5  1  7  8  6  4  2  7  4  5  4  9  3  4
5  4  7  8  1  5  6  1  9  1  7  3  1  1  5
3  4  4  3  2  1  6  6  5  3  9  2  7  8  1
4  6  4  4  7  8  6  2  1  4  3  4  7  8  9
7  1  1  5  4  2  5  6  5  4  3  7  1  9  4
7  8  3  4  3  3  4  5  6  8  7  3  2  4  7
6  6  7  3  1  1  2  5  7  2  3  4  5  5  2
3  3  2  2  7  8  1  9  8  6  5  5  4  1  2
2  1  3  4  3  7  9  1  2  4  5  6  7  8  9
```

Choose a number between 10 and 30.

Find lines of numbers that add to this number.

Example If you choose 17, three ways of adding to 17 are shown.

EXERCISE 4:4

1. Add these numbers.

(a)	(b)	(c)	(d)	(e)	(f)
3	2	9	8	6	7
7	5	2	7	5	4
4	6	1	9	4	9
9	8	7	6	3	6
+ 2	+ 4	+ 3	+ 3	9	5
				+ 8	+ 4

(g) 5 + 4 + 3 + 6 + 2 + 8

(h) 9 + 8 + 6 + 4 + 1 + 6

(i) 9 + 8 + 7 + 3 + 2 + 1

(j) 7 + 1 + 8 + 4 + 3 + 9 + 4

(k) 1 + 2 + 3 + 4 + 5 + 6

(l) 9 + 8 + 7 + 3 + 2 + 1

2. Simon counted the number of each sort
   of fish in a tank.
   This was his list:

   7 3 2 5 9 4 1

   How many fish were in the tank?

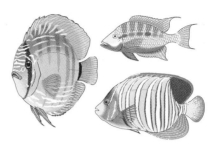

3. On the way home from school, Alison wrote down the number of
   people waiting at bus stops.
   This is her list: 5, 1, 2, 3, 5, 4, 2.

   How many people were waiting altogether?

4. Find the answer to these.

   (a) $8 - 4 + 5 + 6 - 2 + 1$ (b) $7 + 6 - 8 - 1 + 5$

   (c) $2 + 5 - 4 + 9 - 7 - 2$ (d) $9 + 2 + 3 - 4 - 5 - 2$

   (e) $5 + 3 - 2 - 2 - 1$

5. Copy the following.

   Put in + and – signs to make the calculations correct.

   (a) 4 5 6 1 = 2   (b) 7 4 8 = 11   (c) 7 4 2 3 = 10

   (d) 5 2 9 1 = 13   (e) 8 2 3 = 3   (f) 8 1 3 3 = 9

6. Copy this into your book.
   Put + and – signs in the empty circles to make
   each of the six rows correct.

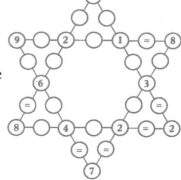

91

Review 1 Add these.

(a) $7 + 5 + 8 + 4 + 6 + 5$ (b) $5 + 9 + 2 + 6 + 8 + 3 + 1$

Review 2 Eva wrote down the number of pets each
of her friends had.
This is her list:
$1, 3, 2, 4, 7, 1, 0$

How many pets did Eva's friends have
altogether?

Review 3 Copy these, then put in + and – signs to make them correct.

(a) 9 1 4 = 12 (b) 4 3 5 6 = 0

PUZZLE 4:5

CLOCK LINES

Two straight lines can be drawn across
this clockface to divide it into three parts.

Where should these lines be drawn if the
sum of the numbers in each of the parts is
to be the same?

INVESTIGATION 4:6

SAME TOTALS

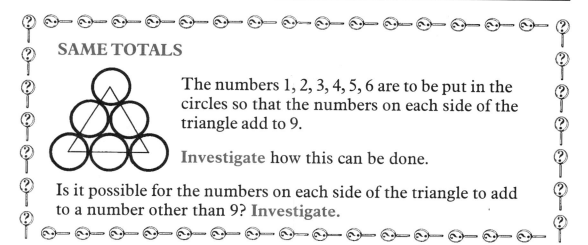

The numbers 1, 2, 3, 4, 5, 6 are to be put in the circles so that the numbers on each side of the triangle add to 9.

Investigate how this can be done.

Is it possible for the numbers on each side of the triangle to add to a number other than 9? **Investigate**.

GAMES 4:7

● **TOTAL "8": a game for 2 players.**

This game begins with a total of 8.
The players take it in turn to subtract 1 or 2.
The first player to get to 0 is the winner.

This is a game of Total "8" that Ann and Barry played. Ann began this game by subtracting 1. Barry won this game.

	Subtract	Total
Start		8
Ann	1	7
Barry	1	6
Ann	2	4
Barry	1	3
Ann	1	2
Barry	2	0

continued . . .

. . . from previous page

● TOTAL "17": a game for 2 players.

This game begins with a total of 0.
The players take it in turn to add 1 or 2 or 3 or 4 to this total.
The first player to reach 17 is the winner.

DISCUSSION 4:8

● Kate and Nicholas add 34 + 18 as follows.

Kate's way: 34 + 10 = 44   44 + 8 = 52 Answer

Nicholas' way: 34   30   4
               + 18   10   8
               ─────   40   12   40 + 12 = 52 Answer 52

Discuss Kate's and Nicholas' ways.

What other ways could you add 34 + 18? **Discuss.**

● Jan used an abacus to add 34 and 18.
Discuss how she could have done this.
Try lots of other additions.

continued . . .

● Eric used a place value table to add 34 and 18.

H	T	O
	3	4
	1 +1	8
	5	2

$4 + 8 = 12$ ones

12 is two ones and 1 ten

$3 + 1 + 1 = 5$

Discuss Eric's way.

Try lots of other additions.

● Kate and Nicholas subtracted 34 – 18 as follows.

Kate's way: $34 - 10 = 24$ $24 - 8 = 16$ Answer

Nicholas' way:
$$\begin{array}{cc} 34 \\ -18 \\ \hline \end{array}$$

| 30 | 4 |
| 10 | 8 |

20	14
10	8
10	6

Answer 16

Discuss Kate's and Nicholas' ways.

Discuss other ways of subtracting.

● Jan used an abacus to work out 34 – 18.
How could she do this? **Discuss.**

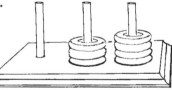

Try these subtractions on the abacus.

49 – 17   64 – 27   86 – 57

● Eric used a place value table to work out 34 – 18.

H	T	O
	2 3	¹4
	1	8
	1	6

Discuss Eric's way.

Try lots of other subtractions.

EXERCISE 4:9

Do not use your calculator for this exercise.

1. Copy and complete these addition tables.

+	18	76	43	24
29				
67				
15				
35				

(a)

+	26		34	81
17				
35		53		
				97
48				

(b)

+	38		24	
71				
		85		59
32				
19		61		

(c)

2. Sue needed 18m of cloth to make wizard outfits and 27m to make fairy outfits for the school play. How much cloth did Sue need altogether?

3. Find

   (a) 87 – 42   (b) 36 – 16   (c) 54 – 28   (d) 68 – 17

   (e) 80 – 29   (f) 47 – 28   (g) 67 – 49   (h) 196 – 67

4. If Mario cycles to school he takes 14 minutes. If he walks to school he takes 33 minutes.

   How much longer does it take Mario to walk rather than cycle to school?

5. What number is 37 less than 91?

6. Derek bought a jacket which cost £27 and a shirt which cost £9.

   How much change did he get from £40?

7. The difference between two numbers is 34.

   (a) If the smaller number is 19, find the larger.

   (b) If the larger is 91, find the smaller.

8. $34 + \bullet = \blacktriangle$ $\qquad$ $\square - 18 = \star$

   Find as many different numbers for $\bullet$, $\blacktriangle$, $\square$, and $\star$ as you can.

Review 1 What number must be added to 37 to make 55?

Review 2 A fox got into a henhouse and ate 13 of the 42 eggs.

   How many eggs were left?

Review 3 An unusual dart board is shown.

   A prize was offered to anyone who could score a total of exactly 100 with five or fewer darts.

   Could this prize be won? If so, which numbers would the darts need to land on?

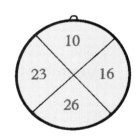

PUZZLE 4:10

MAGIC SQUARE

Copy and fill in this magic square so that each line adds to the same number.

		9	
2	11	7	14
3		6	15
13			1

INVESTIGATION 4:11

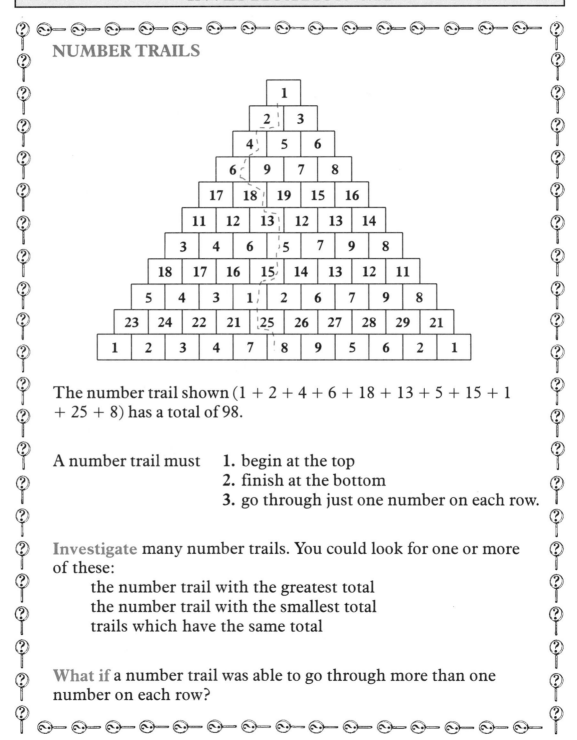

NUMBER TRAILS

The number trail shown (1 + 2 + 4 + 6 + 18 + 13 + 5 + 15 + 1 + 25 + 8) has a total of 98.

A number trail must
1. begin at the top
2. finish at the bottom
3. go through just one number on each row.

Investigate many number trails. You could look for one or more of these:

the number trail with the greatest total
the number trail with the smallest total
trails which have the same total

What if a number trail was able to go through more than one number on each row?

MONEY

DISCUSSION 4:12

-

  Jane buys 5 pencils. How much do these cost? **Discuss** what to press on your calculator to work this out.
  In pounds, one pencil costs £0·23. How many pounds do the 5 pencils cost? **Discuss.**

- Darren had four £1 coins and eight 1p coins. How can we write down how much he had altogether? **Discuss.**

- Baked potatoes cost £1·05. The Brown family bought 5 of these. How much did this cost? **Discuss** what to press on your calculator to work this out.

- Isma asked, "When I work out how much 4 hamburgers cost I get 5·8 on the calculator. Is that five pound and eighty pence or five pound and eight pence?"
  What would your answer be? **Discuss.**

- Five chocolate bars cost £1·05. How much does each cost? How would you work this out using your calculator? **Discuss.**

EXERCISE 4:13

1. Angela worked out the cost of three books. Her calculator showed this.

    $$\boxed{5.04}$$

    Write this in words.

2. Write these in £.

    (a) Fourteen pounds and 10 pence

    (b) Twelve pounds and fifty two pence

    (c) Four pounds and forty pence

    (d) Three pounds and 8 pence

    (e) Eight pounds and 2 pence

    (f) Seventy five pence

3. Trudy has three £1 coins and three 2p coins in her pocket. How much has she got?

4. Jake and Jenny counted the 1p coins they had. They had £1·18. How many 1p coins did they have?

5. A coin trail was made up of fifty one 2p coins. How many £ is this?

6. Dan's father, Dan and his sister went skating. It cost £4 each to skate and £1·80 for food and £2·10 for drinks. How much did it cost altogether?

Review 1　Miranda worked out how much she should pay at the supermarket. Her calculator showed this.

Write this in words.

Review 2　Write five pounds and six pence in £.

Review 3　John and 3 friends went out for lunch for his birthday. They bought 4 pizzas. Each pizza cost £3·10. What was the total cost?

USING the CALCULATOR

When we are given a problem we must decide whether to add, subtract, multiply or divide. Sometimes we need to use the calculator.

Worked Example　Ronan bought 3 drinks at £1·15 each. How much did this cost?

Answer　We have 3 lots of £1·15 so we must **multiply**. It is hard to multiply 3 × 1·15 so we use the calculator. £1·15 is keyed as 1·15.

KEY　3　×　1　·　1　5　=

The calculator shows 3·45.
The drinks cost £3·45.

Worked Example   In a game the first person to get 100 points wins.
Roseanne has 71 points. How many more points does
she need to win?

Answer   She needs to take 71 points away from 100 points.

KEY   ☐1 ☐0 ☐0 ☐− ☐7 ☐1 ☐=

The answer is 29 points.

EXERCISE 4:14

1.   A shop has shoes on display.
There are 4 rows and each row has 8 shoes
on it. How many shoes are there altogether?

2.   Find the cost of

   (a) 4 pizzas at £3·99 each

   (b) 15 books at £2·30 each

   (c) 19 lollies at 5p each

   (d) 5 cards at £1·20 each.

3.   Carmen bought a hamburger for
£1·20 and a Jumbo sausage
and chips for £1·35. How much
did this cost in total?

4. Jacky bought 4 toy cars for her brother Scott's birthday. They were 55p each. How much did these cost altogether?

5. A mini-bus can hold 9 people. How many mini-buses would be needed for 72 people?

6. What is the answer if you subtract 54 from 215 and divide this by 7?

7. Kate and her 4 friends helped shift library books. They carried 13 books each. How many books did they carry altogether?

8. Five sisters shared the cost of a raffle ticket. They won and the prize was £125. How much did each get?

9.

Joshua is saving for headphones. He needs £28. If he saves £3·50 each week, how many weeks will it take him?

10. Aoi bought a shirt for £16·95. She gave a £50 note to pay for it.

   (a) How much change should she get?

   (b) She was given £32·00 change. How much more change should she have got?

11. Todd was paid £7·20 for 4 hours work.

    (a) How much does Todd earn each hour?

    (b) How much would he get for 7 hours work?

12. Melissa multiplies a number by 33 and gets an answer of 792. What was the number?

13. Ranga put 84 into his calculator. He kept subtracting 4 until the answer was zero. How many times did he subtract 4? Write down what he could have done instead of subtracting.

14. Trudy said, "I multiplied two numbers and got 60 as my answer. Guess which two numbers I multiplied." Write down all the possible answers.

Review 1   Alison spent £1·84 on 8 pencils.

    (a) How much did each cost?

    (b) How much would 12 pencils cost?

Review 2   Hunter bought a Lego set for £12·00 and a book for £4·85. How much change did he get from £20?

Review 3   Rebecca multiplied a number by 52 and got 4056. What was the number?

PUZZLE 4:15

● **MULTIPLICATION WHEEL**

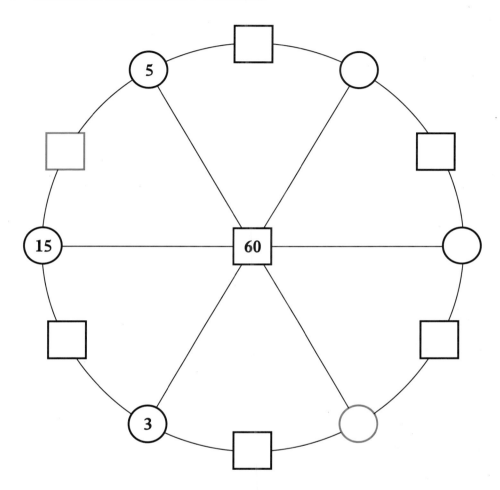

Copy this wheel. The number in each square is found by
multiplying the numbers in the two circles on either side of it.
We can find the number in the red circle by saying
5 × ○ = 60. So the number in the red circle must be 12.
We can find the number in the red box by finding 5 × 15.
Fill in the rest of the multiplication wheel.

● Make up a multiplication wheel of your own.

INVESTIGATION 4:16

3-DIGIT MAGIC

Write down 3 digits. Make all the different 2-digit numbers you can.

If you wrote   **8   5   7**   you can make

85,   87,   57,   58,   75,   78

Add these 2-digit numbers together.

$$85 + 87 + 57 + 58 + 75 + 78 = 440 \quad \text{(1st total)}$$

Add the 3 digits you started with.

$$8 + 5 + 7 = 20 \qquad \text{(2nd total)}$$

Divide the 1st total by the 2nd total.

$$\frac{440}{20} = 22$$

The answer is 22.

Choose another 3-digit number and do the same. What answer do you get? Does this always happen? **Investigate.**

What if the digits you begin with are not all different?

GAME 4:17

DICE TIME – a game for 2 or 3 players

You will need: 3 dice
a timer or watch
a calculator

Toss 3 dice.
Write down the three numbers you get.
Start the timer.
Write down all the 1 and 2-digit numbers you can make with these. Multiply or divide two of these numbers and write down the answer.
Stop the timer after 4 minutes.
For instance if you tossed

you can make   2,   3,   4,   23,   24,   32,   34,   42,   43

to give

$2 \times 3 = 6$	$3 \times 4 = 12$	$24 \div 3 = 8$	$32 \div 4 = 8$
$2 \times 4 = 8$	$3 \times 23 = 69$	$42 \div 2 = 21$	$34 \div 2 = 17$
$2 \times 23 = 46$	$3 \times 24 = 72$	$32 \div 2 = 16$	$23 \times 24 = 552$

and many more.

Check each other's answers.
Take one point for each right answer and subtract one point for each wrong answer.
The winner is the person who has the most points.

INVESTIGATION 4:18

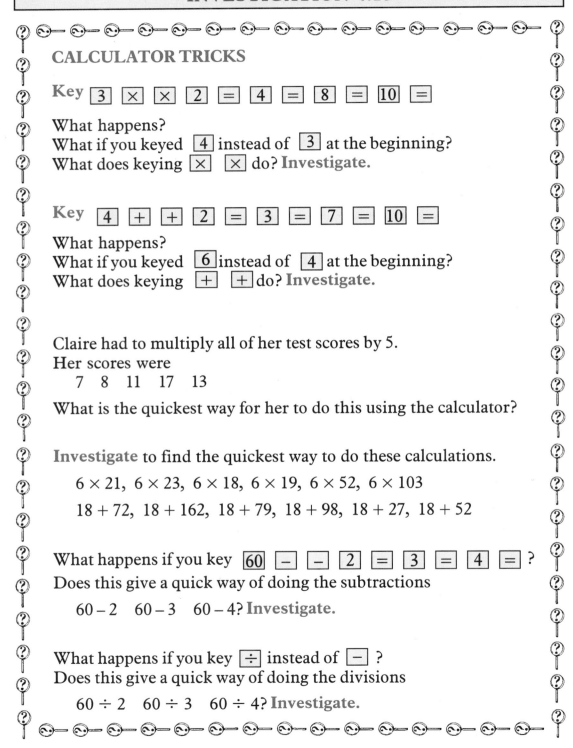

CALCULATOR TRICKS

Key [3] [×] [×] [2] [=] [4] [=] [8] [=] [10] [=]

What happens?
What if you keyed [4] instead of [3] at the beginning?
What does keying [×] [×] do? **Investigate.**

Key [4] [+] [+] [2] [=] [3] [=] [7] [=] [10] [=]

What happens?
What if you keyed [6] instead of [4] at the beginning?
What does keying [+] [+] do? **Investigate.**

Claire had to multiply all of her test scores by 5.
Her scores were
    7   8   11   17   13
What is the quickest way for her to do this using the calculator?

Investigate to find the quickest way to do these calculations.

    6×21, 6×23, 6×18, 6×19, 6×52, 6×103

    $18 + 72$, $18 + 162$, $18 + 79$, $18 + 98$, $18 + 27$, $18 + 52$

What happens if you key [60] [−] [−] [2] [=] [3] [=] [4] [=] ?
Does this give a quick way of doing the subtractions

    $60 - 2$ $60 - 3$ $60 - 4$? **Investigate.**

What happens if you key [÷] instead of [−] ?
Does this give a quick way of doing the divisions

    $60 \div 2$ $60 \div 3$ $60 \div 4$? **Investigate.**

WORK THIS OUT

1.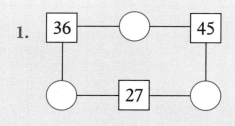

The number in a box is made by adding the numbers in the circles on either side of the box. Find the numbers that go in the circles.

2.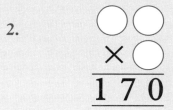

Put 3 different digits in the circles so that the answer is 170. Is there more than one answer?

Look Around You at . . .

The Supermarket

PRACTICAL AND DISCUSSION 5:1

- Make a list of 20 things you can buy at the supermarket. About
    - how much would they cost in total
    - how much would they weigh in total
    - how much time would it take to shop for them?

  Discuss this with your group.

- Bring some packets or jars to school. Look at the labels. Do you think the amount written on the packet will be the *EXACT* amount inside? **Discuss.**

- "It's best to work out about how much your shopping is going to cost before you get to the checkout," said Brian. How could you do this? **Discuss.**

ROUNDING UP or DOWN. REMAINDERS.

DISCUSSION 5:2

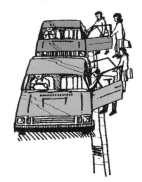

- How many cars would be needed to take your class on a journey if each car could take 4? **Discuss.** Would there be any spare seats? **Discuss.**

- How many rows of desks would your classroom have if each row had 5 desks in it? **Discuss.** Would every row be full? **Discuss.**

- How many buses, each holding 40 people, would be needed to take your school on a journey? **Discuss.** How many spare seats would there be? **Discuss.**

 How many desks could you put along one wall of your classroom? **Discuss.** Would there be any space left over? **Discuss.**

- Pizzas cost £5·50. If each person in your class brought a £1 coin to school, how many pizzas could you buy? **Discuss.** Would there be any money left over? **Discuss.**

Worked Example   Books in a sale cost £5.

(a) How many books can Tim buy with £18?

(b) How much money will Tim have left?

Answer   (a) We want to know how many lots of £5 there are in £18.

On the calculator 18 ÷ 5 =    3.6

Tim can only buy 3 books.

(b) $3 \times 5 = 15$. 3 books cost £15.
 $18 - 15 = 3$. Tim will have £3 left.

Worked Example   Eggs are packed in boxes of 6.

(a) How many boxes would be needed for 27 eggs?

(b) How many more eggs could be packed?

Answer   (a) 27 ÷ 6 =   4.5

If we have 4 boxes there will be some eggs left unpacked.
We need 5 boxes to pack all the eggs.

(b) $5 \times 6 = 30$. We could pack 30 eggs altogether. We have
27 eggs so 3 more eggs could be packed.

EXERCISE 5:3

1. Ross was saving for a Sega game which cost £14. He saved £3 each month. How many months would it take him?

2.
    Balloons were being tied in lots of 3 for a fair.

    (a) How many lots of 3 could be made from 41 balloons?

    (b) How many balloons would be left?

3. Cans of drink come in 6-packs.

    (a) How many 6-packs are needed for 28 people?

    (b) How many cans are left over?

4. Tickets to a show cost £6.

    (a) How many could be bought for £26?

    (b) How much money is left?

5.
    3 people fit on a seat.

    (a) How many seats are needed for 22 people?

    (b) How many more people could sit down?

6. Lucy shared 25 chocolates with her 3 friends.
   They all got the same number of chocolates.

   (a) How many chocolates did each get?

   (b) How many chocolates were left over?

7. Find the remainder.

   (a) 17 ÷ 4   (b) 25 ÷ 3   (c) 19 ÷ 4   (d) 27 ÷ 6

   (e) 37 ÷ 6   (f) 31 ÷ 5   (g) 23 ÷ 7   (h) 35 ÷ 4

8. Mateen divides a number by 6. The answer is 8 and the remainder is 2.
   What is the number?

9. *The remainder is 3.* Make up some divisions which have a remainder
   of 3.

Review 1 27 people are put into 4 tug-of-war teams. Each team has the
   same number of people.

   (a) How many are in each team?

   (b) How many people are left over?

Review 2 The Turner family need 21 litres of paint to paint their house.

   If paint comes in 4 litre tins

   (a) how many tins will be needed

   (b) how many litres of paint will be left?

DISCUSSION 5:4

If you had £10 what would you choose to do with it? Discuss.

INVESTIGATION 5:5

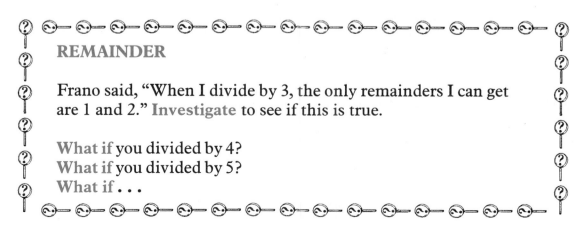

REMAINDER

Frano said, "When I divide by 3, the only remainders I can get are 1 and 2." Investigate to see if this is true.

What if you divided by 4?
What if you divided by 5?
What if . . .

GAME 5:6

LEFT OVERS — a game for 2 players

You will need: a die
                    10 blue counters for one person
                    10 red counters for the other
                    the board below

3	4	5	6	7	8
9	10	11	12	13	14
15	16	17	18	19	20
21	22	23	24	25	26
27	28	29	30	31	32
33	34	35	36	37	38

continued . . .

. . . from previous page

Take turns to

1. Toss the die. This is your remainder.

2. Divide 2, 3, 4, 5, 6 or 7 into one of the numbers on the board to get the remainder shown on the die.

    Example

    If you toss you need a remainder of 3.

    You could divide 4 into 15 to get remainder of 3.

3. Put a counter on the number used on the board. That is, put a counter on 15 for this example.

3	4	5	6	7	8
9	10	11	12	13	14
15	16	17	18	19	20
21	22	23	24	25	26
27	28	29	30	31	32
33	34	35	36	37	38

Note: If you cannot make your remainder, it is the other person's turn. The winner is the person with the most counters on the board after 10 turns each.

INVESTIGATION 5:7

STAMPS

You have 1p, 2p and 5p stamps. Can you send a 43p parcel using these stamps? **Investigate** all the possible costs of parcels, up to £1, you can send using these stamps.

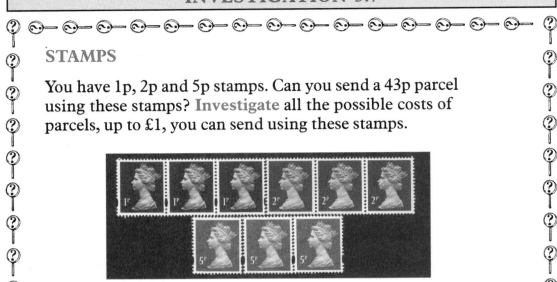

INVESTIGATION 5:8

SEATING PLANS

35 people are coming to watch your class play. Each row must have fewer than 9 chairs. How many different ways can you set out the chairs? **Investigate.**

What if you had 30 people coming?
What if each row must have fewer than 10 chairs?
What if . . . (make up some numbers of your own for the number of people coming and the number of chairs in each row).

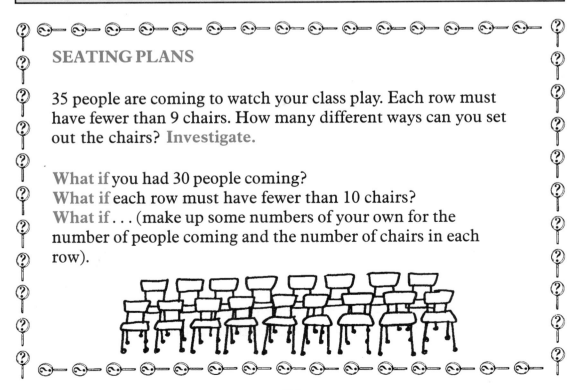

ROUNDING to the NEAREST 10 or 100

DISCUSSION 5:9

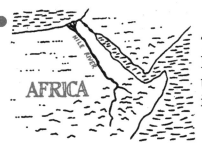

● The longest river in the world is the Nile. It is 6670 km long. Which digit tells us most about how long the Nile is? **Discuss.**

● There are fewer than 1000 smarties in the jar. You are allowed to ask what *one* of the digits is before you guess. Which digit would you ask for, the hundreds digit, the tens digit or the ones digit? Why? **Discuss.**

GUESS HOW MANY SMARTIES

●

Is 67 closer to 60 or 70? **Discuss.**
What about 62, 64, 69? Which is each of these closest to? **Discuss.**

●

Is 430 closer to 400 or 500? **Discuss.**
What about 470, 435, 487? Which is each of these closest to? **Discuss.**

Sometimes we **round** numbers. To round to the **nearest ten**, we find the tens which are closest to the number.

36 is between 30 and 40.

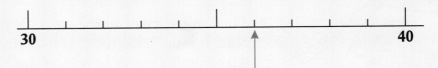

36 is closer to 40 than to 30.
36 rounded to the nearest ten is 40.

To round to the **nearest hundred** we find the hundreds that are closest to the number.

824 is between 800 and 900.

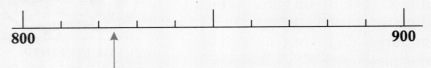

824 is closer to 800 than to 900.
824 rounded to the nearest hundred is 800.

If the number is halfway between, we round up.

35 is halfway between 30 and 40.
35 to the nearest ten is 40.

850 is halfway between 800 and 900.
850 to the nearest hundred is 900.

Worked Example   There are 882 people at a concert. How many is this

(a) to the nearest ten

(b) to the nearest hundred?

Answer   (a)

882 is between 880 and 890.
882 is closer to 880 than to 890.
882 rounded to the nearest ten is 880.

(b)

882 is between 800 and 900.
882 is closer to 900 than to 800.
882 rounded to the nearest hundred is 900.

EXERCISE 5:10

1.

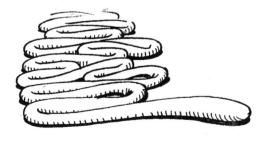

The longest sausage ever made was 21km long. How long is this to the nearest ten kilometres?

2. The tallest lamppost is in France. It is 64m tall. How tall is this to the nearest ten metres?

3. Mehmet had 287 stamps. How many is this to the nearest ten?

4. Round these to the nearest ten.

    (a) 57   (b) 65   (c) 11   (d) 8   (e) 124

    (f) 179   (g) 345   (h) 104   (i) 1398   (j) 1864

5. A school had a roll of 479. What is this to the nearest hundred?

6. The cost of some mountain bikes is given in the table.
    Copy the table. Round each price to the nearest £100.

MOUNTAIN BIKE	COST	ROUNDED TO NEAREST £100
CHEETAH	£249	
PANTHA	£439	
ROCKET XT	£399	
ROCKET BN	£169	
FASTRAX A	£507	
FASTRAX B	£633	

7. Round these to the nearest hundred.

    (a) 830   (b) 590   (c) 417   (d) 650   (e) 795

    (f) 250   (g) 389   (h) 502   (i) 74   (j) 46

8. A number rounded to the nearest ten is 50. Find all the numbers this could be.

9. The number of people at a football match is 900, to the nearest hundred.

   (a) What is the largest number of people that could have been there?

   (b) What is the smallest number of people that could have been there?

Review 1

The largest "lived in" castle in the world is Windsor Castle. It is 576m long and 164m wide. Round these to the nearest ten metres.

Review 2 Catherine counted the number of peas in a packet of dried peas. There were 879. Round this to the nearest hundred.

PRACTICAL 5:11

Collect numbers about your class and school.
You might collect
  — the number in each class
  — the number in your school
  — the number that play each sport
  — the amount of water (in litres) to fill a sink.

Round these numbers to the nearest 10 or the nearest 100. You will need to decide which is best. Make a poster, collage or mural to show what you found.

GAME 5:12

ROUNDUP — a game for 2 players.

You will need 3 dice
a coin
red counters for 1 player, blue for the other
the board on the next page

1. Toss 3 dice. Write down all the 3-digit numbers you can make. You may not use a digit twice.

Example If you toss 2, 3 and 6 you can make 236, 263, 326, 362, 632, 623.

2. Toss a coin. If it is heads, round the 3-digit numbers to the nearest 10. If it is tails round the 3-digit numbers to the nearest 100.

Example If you toss a tail the numbers you made in **1.** would be rounded to 200, 300, 300, 400, 600, 600.

3. Place a counter on each square which has a number you made in **2.**

For the example above, counters would be placed on 200, 300, 400 and 600.

continued . . .

. . . *from previous page*

100	510	200	320	300	610	700	410
300	270	100	400	110	100	200	600
600	400	430	300	520	210	200	340
370	530	500	150	100	420	500	650
350	400	200	120	100	640	170	540
500	440	220	300	460	660	700	230
700	200	670	260	550	130	250	500
140	600	310	200	330	620	300	400
400	100	300	560	240	450	360	600
700	600	570	160	700	500	630	470

The winner is the person with the most counters on the board after 6 turns each.

CHECKING CALCULATIONS

DISCUSSION 5:13

$$38 + 57 = 85$$

"I knew the answer was wrong because I did the calculation again", said Nelson.

"I knew it was wrong because I checked it by adding 57 + 38", said Becky.

"I knew it was wrong because 38 is about 40 and 57 is about 60 so the answer should be close to 100", said Bret.

Discuss the ways Nelson, Becky and Bret checked the answer.

If we use a calculator we don't need to check the answer.

Is this true? Discuss.

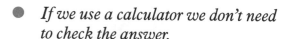

28 + 46 = 46 + 28   52 − 38 = 14
32 × 21 = 21 × 32   66 ÷ 22 = 3

We can check addition and multiplication by doing them in a different order.

How can we check subtraction and division? Discuss.

Always **check your answers** even when using the calculator.

EXERCISE 5:14

1.

1.	2.	3.	4.
$29+33=62$	$30\times4=120$	$86+29=105$	$79-16=63$
5.	**6.**	**7.**	**8.**
$72\times3=216$	$54+28=82$	$73-56=17$	$49+21=60$
9.	**10.**	**11.**	**12.**
$200\div50=4$	$41\times7=327$	$55-27=28$	$42\times5=210$
13.	**14.**	**15.**	**16.**
$50\times5=250$	$83-27=66$	$52\div4=14$	$86+17=103$
17.	**18.**	**19.**	**20.**
$500\div20=25$	$29+28=57$	$400\div5=8$	$32\times6=192$

The answers to six of these calculations are wrong. Which boxes have the wrong answers?

2. Do these calculations and check them.

   (a) $86 - 27$ (b) $32 + 89$ (c) 7×9 (d) $81 \div 9$

   (e) $5 + 9 + 8 + 4 + 6$ (f) $27 + 32 - 19$

3.

At a Christmas party each child got three chocolate Santas. Alfred worked out that he would need 91 Santas for 27 children. Was he right? If not, how many Santas were needed?

4. Jane used the calculator to work out 78×52.
   She got an answer of 1·5. How could she tell without checking that this was wrong?

Review   Andrew did four calculations for homework. Check if Andrew's calculations are right or wrong. Give the right answers for those he got wrong.

   (a) $58 - 39 = 29$ (b) $84 + 26 = 100$

   (c) $7 \times 7 = 49$ (d) $100 \div 5 = 25$

WORK THIS OUT

A roller-coaster takes 14 people. One ride takes 7 minutes. If you are waiting for the roller-coaster and there are 83 people in front of you, how long will you have to wait?

Temperatures

DISCUSSION AND PRACTICAL 6:1

- There are some places in the world where the temperature is always below zero. What does below zero mean? What do you think life would be like there? **Discuss.**
  Make a poster, collage, mural or give a talk on "Life At Below Zero."

- Collect temperatures of cities around the world from the newspaper. Make a chart of these.

USING NEGATIVE NUMBERS

DISCUSSION 6:2

● **CITY FROZE LAST NIGHT IN -12°C**

Last night was the coldest since 1941. The temperature went to -12°C. Many old peo without heating. The central blankets

What does –12°C mean? Discuss.

●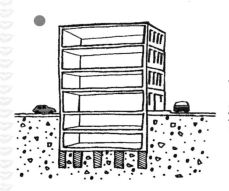

What numbers could be used for the ground floor, 1st basement and 2nd basement? Discuss.

● Jennifer bought a computer game for £28. After 3 weeks she sold it to a friend for £19. Jennifer put 19 – 28 into her calculator. What answer did she get? What does this mean? Discuss.

Think of other calculations you might do on the calculator where the answer would be negative. Discuss.

continued . . .

. . . from previous page

● The top of the boat's mast is 30 metres above sea level. We could write this as +30m.

What numbers could be used to show where the diver and the fish are? **Discuss.**

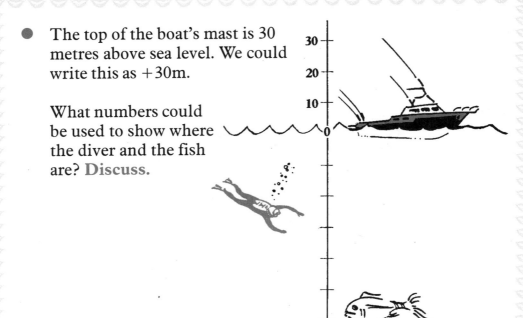

● Sometimes people spend more money than they have in the bank. The bank sends them a letter telling them they are **overdrawn.** This is written as **OD** beside the amount. Frances was told she was £15·00 OD.
How could we write this using a negative number? **Discuss.**

	STATEMENT DATE 22 OCT 1993		ACCOUNT NO. 81905254
WITHDRAWALS		DEPOSITS	BALANCE (£)
			526.33 OD
10.00			536.33 OD

● Think of other places where you might use negative numbers. **Discuss.**

We often use **negative numbers** as well as positive numbers.
The number –2 is a negative number.   –2 means 2 less than zero.

This shows the temperature –5°C. This is 5° below zero.

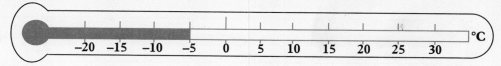

Sometimes the answers to calculations are negative.

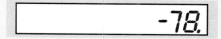

We can show negative *and* positive numbers on a number line.

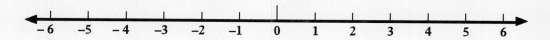

EXERCISE 6:3

1.   What temperature is shown?

(a)

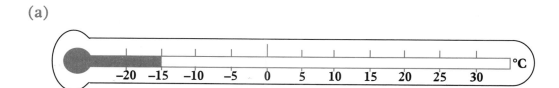

(b)

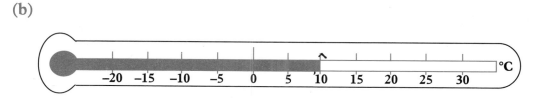

(c)

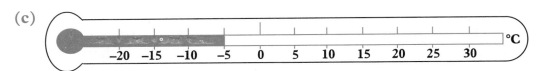

(d)

2. What level is the water at?

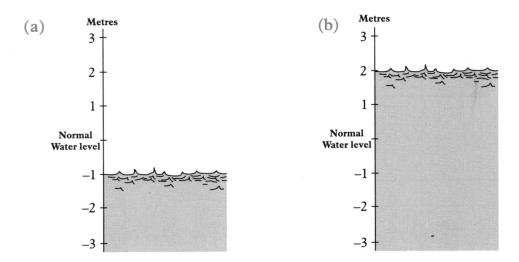

3. This is a dial on a freezer. What do the pointers read?

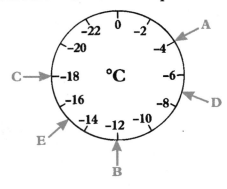

4. At high tide the water is 40cm above its normal level. This is shown as 40. What number would you use to show a low tide of 25cm below normal?

5. Write these temperatures as a positive or negative number.

London	5°C
Edinburgh	3°C below zero
Aberdeen	5°C below zero
Iceland	15°C below zero

6. The bank kept a list of bank balances. Copy this list and write the balance as a positive or negative number.

Thom	£542
Thomas	£78 OD
Thompson	£678
Thoms	£342 OD
Thorn	£52 OD
Thornton	£4
Thorp	£87 OD

7. Joanne was saving for a CD player which cost £149. She had saved £107. She did a calculation on her calculator and got – 42.

$$-42.$$

(a) What calculation did she do?

(b) Explain what – 42 means.

8. Make up a story for the calculation 54 – 79.

9.

E   C   B   D   A

What number is at

(a) A   (b) B   (c) C   (d) D   (e) E ?

10. On Feb 6 1993 a temperature of – 68°C was recorded in Siberia. Which of these shows this?

A.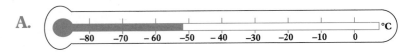

B.

C.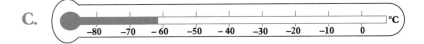

D.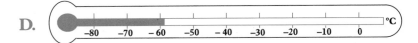

Review 1   What temperature does this show?

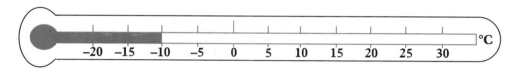

Review 2   Write these as positive or negative numbers.

(a) 8°C below zero

(b) 20cm above normal water level

(c) £80 OD

(d) 50cm below normal water level

Review 3   Shadia was to spend 40 minutes on her homework. She had spent 23 minutes. Shadia did a calculation on her calculator and got −17.

(a) What calculation did Shadia do?

(b) What does −17 mean?

Review 4

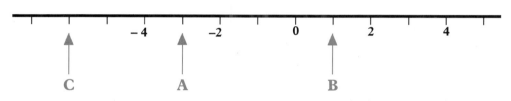

What number is at   (a) A   (b) B   (c) C ?

GAME 6:4

♥ LUCKY GOLD – a game for 2 players

You will need: 13 markers – you could use chalk marks, paper or chairs.
a cube (or die)

First

On the 6 faces of a cube write the numbers
1, 2, 3, –1, –2, and –3.

The Game

In an old fairy story, a rich King played a game with his people. Each person who played had a chance to win gold. The King had a staircase with 13 steps. The person began on the middle step. There were 6 steps up to the gold and 6 steps down to a door. The King tossed a die with 1, 2, 3 and –1, –2, –3 on it. The person would move up and down the staircase.

If the person reached the door at the bottom the game was over and they didn't get any gold. If the person reached the top, he or she was given gold.

continued . . .

. . . from previous page

Play this game by marking 13 steps. One person is the King and tosses the die, the other begins on the middle step.

If 2 is tossed the person moves up 2.
If −3 is tossed the person moves down 3, and so on.

If the gold is reached the person is a winner. If the door at the bottom is reached it is the other player's turn.

WORK THIS OUT

1. In a race, some horses were given a head start and others started behind the line. Racer had a head start of 8 metres. Ziggy started 6 metres behind the line. When Ziggy crossed the finish line Racer had 5 metres to go. If the race was 500 metres long how far did each horse run? How far had Racer run when Ziggy crossed the finish line?

2. Mr Graham had £350 in the bank. He owed his friend £500. He put some more money in the bank and paid his friend. He now had £50 more in the bank than at first. How much did he put in the bank?

1. Write the following in words.

    (a) 582   (b) 1806   (c) 4009   (d) 6832

    (e) 503   (f) 7080   (g) 4300   (h) 6894

2.

H			C			S	
28	75	54	195	468		325	872

ON		H			M	
	964	905	844		555	768

Copy the box. Look at the number under each line.
If the number is divisible by 5 put an A above the line.
If the number is divisible by 2 put a T above the line.
What does it say?

3. What is the missing number?

    (a) $8 + 9 = \square$ (b) $9 + 6 = \square$ (c) $11 + \square = 16$

    (d) $19 - \square = 8$ (e) $17 - \square = 0$ (f) $20 - \square = 14$

    (g) $5 \times 4 = \square$ (h) $3 \times \square = 12$ (i) $10 \times \square = 70$

    (j) $9 \times \square = 45$ (k) $30 \div 5 = \square$ (l) $18 \div 3 = \square$

    (m) $25 \div \square = 5$ (n) $80 \div \square = 10$ (o) $\square \div 5 = 7$

4. If this pattern carries on, what will be above 21?

✖	❈	✖	✖	❈	❈	✖	✖	✖	❈	❈	❈
1	2	3	4	5	6	7	8	9	10	11	12

5. Copy these and fill in the boxes.

(a) $27 + 9 = 27 + 10 - \square$
       $= \square$

(b) $63 - 8 = 63 - 10 + \square$
       $= \square$

6. Write in figures.

(a) Nine thousand three hundred and twenty seven

(b) Four hundred and two

(c) Three thousand and four

(d) 3 thousands and 5 tens and 4 ones

(e) 8 thousands and four ones

(f) Six thousands and two hundreds

7. Write a number pattern for these.

(a)

(b)

(c) Write down the next number for the number pattern in (b).

142

8. Morgan worked out that he needed to save £5 each week for 13 weeks to buy a cycle for £75.
Check Morgan's calculation. Was he right? If not, how many weeks will it take him if he saves £5 each week?

9. Copy this chart. Fill it in. The first row has been done for you.

Number	Thousands	Hundreds	Tens	Ones
1053	1		5	3
536				
21				
1340				
1009				
407				
5				

10. (a) What place value does 7 have in each of the numbers?

487 people win prizes this week

7500 **at football**

This footbridge will hold 780kg (maximum)

(b) How many people each weighing 60kg could stand on the footbridge?

11. Write down the next 3 lines of these.

(a) $9 + 8 = 17$
$19 + 8 = 27$
$29 + 8 = 37$

(b) $5 \times 1 = 5$
$5 \times 2 = 10$
$5 \times 3 = 15$

(c) $7 + 4 = 11$
$8 + 4 = 12$
$9 + 4 = 13$

(d) Write about the patterns in (a), (b), and (c) in your own words.

12.

35	27	149	301	682	455	753
47	73	20	84	76	25	1035
191	150	300	875	934	932	540
239	91	70	42	683	874	360
841	107	960	50	140	80	412
79	234	200	410	270	90	901
114	657	1040	57	713	1430	3412
17	435	890	82	9	1200	864

Copy this box. Shade the numbers which are divisible by 10.
What picture did you find?

13. Lisa bought 15 cakes. Each cake cost 22p. How much did they cost altogether?

14. Copy these patterns. Put the next 15 dots on each.

(a) ● ● ● ● ● ● ● ● ● ● ● ● ● ● ● ● ● ●

(b) ● · ● · ● ● ● ● ● ● ● ● ● ● ● ● ● ● ● ● ● · ● ● · ● ●

15. Which of these sentences are true?

    (a) Numbers which end with a 5 or a 0 are divisible by 5.

    (b) Numbers which end with a 5 or a 0 are divisible by 10.

    (c) Numbers which end with an even number are divisible by 2.

    (d) Numbers which end with a 0 are divisible by 5 and 2 and 10.

    (e) Numbers which end with an even number are divisible by 10.

16. Multiply each of the numbers on the wheel by the number in the middle.

    (a)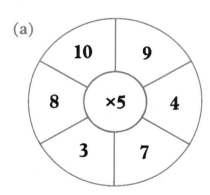

    (b)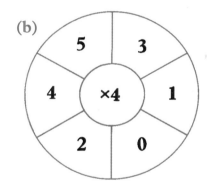

17. Rick spent £2·70 on 5 packets of sweets.

    (a) How much did each packet cost?

    (b) Rick also bought some chocolates for £1·60. How much did this cost altogether?

18. Jennifer has four £1 coins and eight 1p coins. How much money is this?

145

19. Which number is 452 closer to, 400 or 500?

20. There are 24 sweets in a packet.

    (a) How many sweets are there in 5 packets?

    (b) Jill bought some packets. She had 72 sweets.
        How many packets did she buy?

    (c) To the nearest ten, how many sweets did Jill have?

21. Copy and fill in the gaps.

    (a) $47 + 39 = 40 +$ ____ $+ 30 +$ ____   (b) $15 \times 9 = 10 \times$ ____ $+ 5 \times$ ____
    $= 40 +$ ____ $+ 7 +$ ____ $\qquad\qquad = $ ____ $+$ ____
    $=$ ____ $+$ ____ $\qquad\qquad\qquad\qquad = $ ____ $+ 40 +$ ____
    $=$ ____ $+ 10 +$ ____ $\qquad\qquad\quad = $ ____ $+$ ____
    $=$ ____ $+$ ____ $\qquad\qquad\qquad\qquad = $ ____
    $=$ ____

22. Cliff and Jill saved for a show in London.
    Cliff saved £53 and Jill saved £49.

    Without using the calculator:

    (a) Work out how much Cliff and Jill had saved altogether.

    (b) The show cost £90 for the two. How much did they have left
        altogether?

GLENFIELD SCHOOL
presents
"MASKED BALL"
14th–16th Sept
at 7pm

Tickets £3.

23. (a) How many tickets could Tony buy for £14?

(b) Tickets worth £567 were sold.
How many tickets was this?

24. This chart shows the week's sales for four shops.

SALES	
Name of Shop	**£**
Fancy That	1847
Up to Date	1869
Friends Fashion	1896
Today	1930

(a) Which shop had the highest sales?

(b) Which shop had the next highest?

(c) Which shop sold the least?

(d) Round each amount to the nearest £100.

25.

$$-4 \qquad 0 \quad 1 \qquad 4$$

Copy this number line. Put these numbers on it.

$$-2 \qquad -7 \qquad 3 \qquad -1 \qquad 2 \qquad -5$$

26. Explain why three hundred and two is not written as 32.

27. What is the next number in these number patterns?

(a) 3, 6, 9, 12, . . .   (b) 50, 48, 46, 44, . . .

(c) 1, 3, 9, 27, . . .   (d) 4, 2, 2, 8, 2, 2, 16, 2, 2, . . .

(e) 5, 6, 8, 11, 15, . . .   (f) 2, 10, 4, 20, 6, 30, . . .

28. What is the reading on these?

(a)

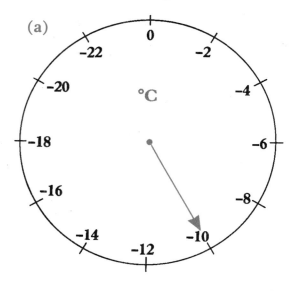

(b)

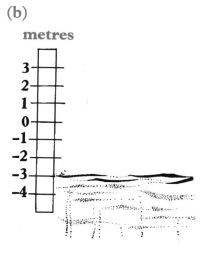

(c)

29. Copy this sentence and fill in the gaps.

If a number is divisible by   and   it is always divisible by 10.

30. A lift is taking people up to a tearooms on the top floor.

    (a) How many trips will be needed for 97 people?

    (b) Explain your answer to (a).

31. There are 19 people on a bus.

    (a) At the first stop, 8 people get off. How many people are left on the bus?

    (b) At the next stop 5 people get on and 3 get off. How many people are on the bus now?

32.

F	I	N	D	F	I	N	D	F	I	N	...
1	3	5	7	9	11	13	15	17	19	21	...

    (a) Which letter will be above 29?

    (b) Which letter will be above 43?

33. Jane was having an end-of-year party. She made an estimate of the number of people coming. Would she be better to underestimate or overestimate. Explain your answer.

34. Put < or > between the two numbers.

    (a) 582   852   (b) 325   327   (c) 471   465

    (d) 1427   1423   (e) 3271   3275   (f) 1890   1909

35. At a fair, a ride on "Hunters Trail" is £2·50. Belinda loves this ride and wants to spend all of her money on it. She has £11.

    (a) How many rides can Belinda have?

    (b) How much money will she have left?

36. $30 \times 1 = 30$ $1 \times 30 = 30$

These are 2 ways to make 30. Copy the box below and fill it in with 6 other ways to make 30.

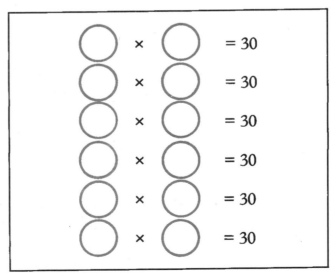

37. *The remainder is 3.* Write down 4 divisions which have a remainder of 3.

38. Give the numbers in these sentences to the nearest 10.

(a) The tallest building in the world is the Sears Tower in Chicago. It is 443m high.

(b) The longest tunnel in the world is a water tunnel in New York. It is 169km long.

(c) The longest ears on a rabbit were on an English Lop rabbit. They were 73cm long.

(d) The largest Easter egg ever made was about as heavy as an elephant. It weighed 4755kg.

39. Give the numbers in the sentences in **question 38** to the nearest 100.

40. Edward needed 48m of material to make the curtains for the school play. He had 23m. He did a calculation on the calculator and got –25.

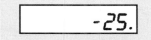

(a) What calculation did Edward do?

(b) What does this answer mean?

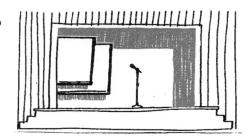

41. Write down the next 2 pairs of this pattern.

$$3 \times 4 = 12 \qquad 3 \times 5 = 15$$
$$6 \times 4 = 24 \qquad 6 \times 5 = 30$$

42. Without using the calculator, find

    (a) $7 + 8 + 6 + 3 + 9 + 2$ (b) $8 + 6 - 3 + 4 - 2$ (c) $96 - 59$

    (d) $84 + 37$ (e) $56 - 18$ (f) $127 - 94$

43. Julian tossed 3 dice and got a four, a two and a six. What three-digit numbers can he make with these? Put the three-digit numbers in order from smallest to largest.

44. How many ways can you make 10 using the numbers 1, 2, 3, 4, 5, 6 and 7 and + and − ? You may not use any number twice in a sentence. You may not use + or − twice in a sentence.

45. Belinda said, "I have 3 coins in my pocket and they are all different." What might these coins be? Think of as many answers as you can.

46. $\square - 23 = \triangle$.
    Find as many numbers as you can for $\square$ and $\triangle$.

SHAPE, SPACE and MEASURES

Shape, Space and Measures from Previous Levels

SHAPES

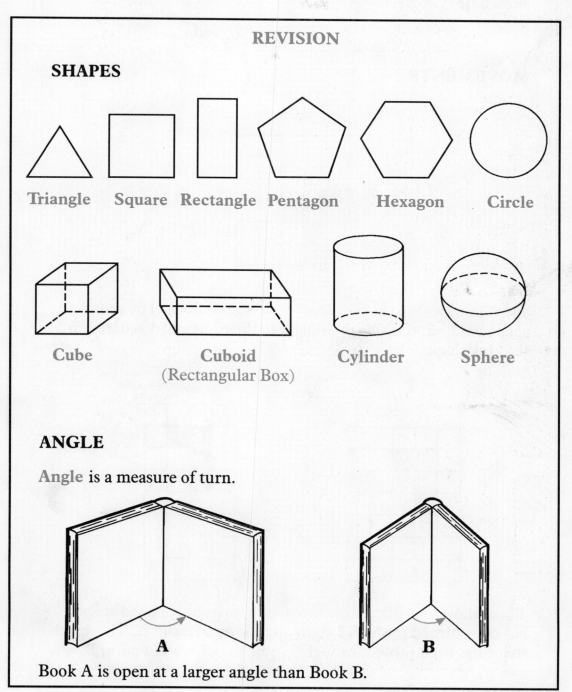

Triangle   Square   Rectangle   Pentagon   Hexagon   Circle

Cube   Cuboid (Rectangular Box)   Cylinder   Sphere

ANGLE

Angle is a measure of turn.

A   B

Book A is open at a larger angle than Book B.

continued . . .

. . . *from previous page*

A **right angle** is a quarter of a full turn. We use a small square written in the angle to show a right angle.

MOVEMENTS

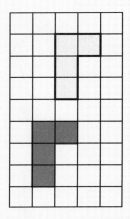

This shows a **straight movement (or translation)**. The red shape has been translated 1 square to the right and 4 squares up to the grey shape.

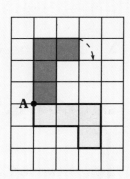
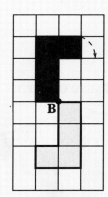

These show a **turning movement (or rotation)**. The red shape has been turned through 1 right angle around point A. The black shape has been turned through 2 right angles around point B.

continued . . .

MEASURES

Metres (m) and kilometres (km) and miles are used to measure **length**.

Kilograms (kg) and pounds (lb) are used to measure **weight**.

Litres (*l* or L) and pints are used to measure how much water a container will hold.

Years, weeks, days, hours and minutes are used to measure **time**.
There are 7 days in one week and 52 weeks in a year.
There are 365 days in a year but in a leap year there are 366 days.
There are 24 hours in a day. There are 60 minutes in one hour.

REVISION EXERCISE

1.

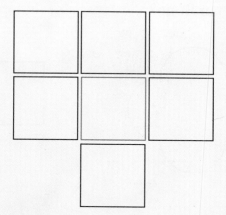

Copy these boxes.

Put a ● in the red box.

Put a ✓ in the box above the red one.

Put an **X** in the box below the red one.

Put a ★ in the box on the left of the red one.

2. To measure how tall a building is you would use

   A. kilometres   **B.** miles   **C.** metres   **D.** kilograms.

3.

CHLOE

BLACKIE

BONO

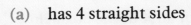
DIGGER

(a) Which dog is the tallest?

(b) Which dog has the shortest legs?

(c) Which dog has a longer nose than Chloe?

(d) Which dog has a shorter tail than Bono?

4. Which shape

(a) has 4 straight sides

(b) has a pointed end

(c) has all curved sides

(d) is round?

A.

B.

C.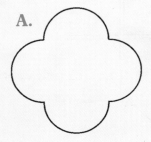

D.

5.

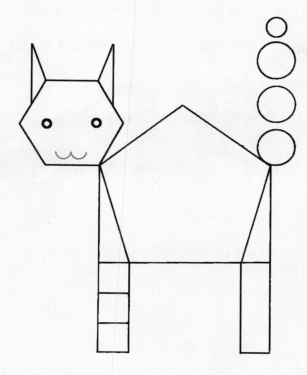

Write about this picture. Write about the shapes in it and where they are in the picture.

6. Sevenoaks School had an obstacle course. Mrs Patel put a sign at each obstacle.

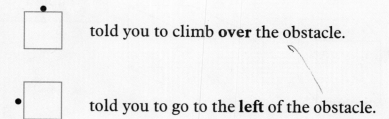

What do you think these cards mean?

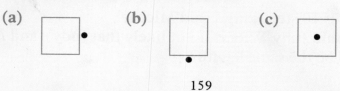

7. The amount of petrol in a car would be measured in

   A. kilograms   **B.** litres   **C.** metres   **D.** kilometres.

8. Use a word from the box to name these shapes.

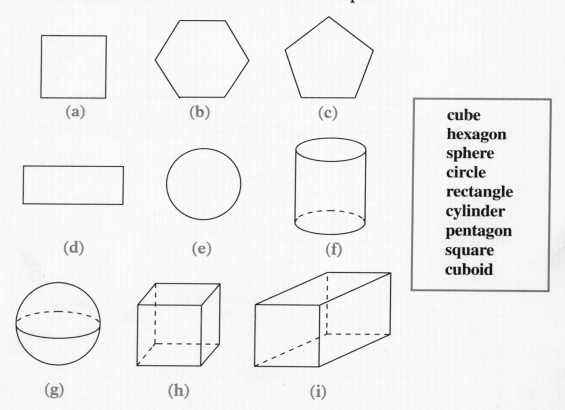

(a)   (b)   (c)

cube
hexagon
sphere
circle
rectangle
cylinder
pentagon
square
cuboid

(d)   (e)   (f)

(g)   (h)   (i)

9. "My bedroom is 10 steps long," said Michael.
   "So is mine," said Judy. Why is it not likely that Judy's and Michael's bedrooms will be the same length?

160

10.

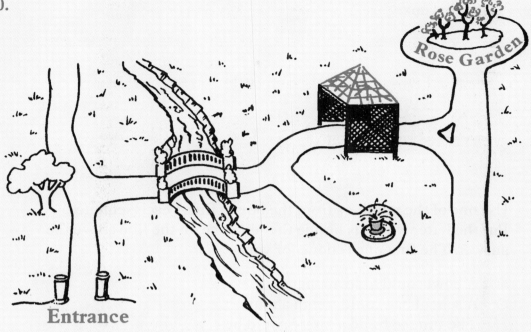

Entrance

Paula wants to get to the Rose Garden in the park. Finish these directions to tell Paula where to go.

Walk in the entrance.
At the big tree turn right.

11. Some of the corners in these shapes have a letter next to them. Which of these corners are right-angled corners?

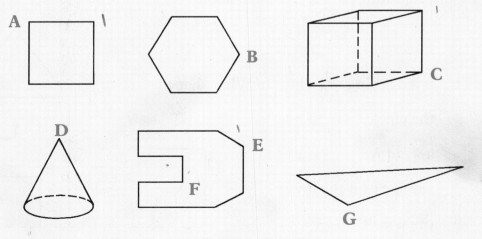

161

12. Copy this box.

6 months	300km	6 hours		1 pound	$\frac{1}{2}$ metre	2kg	16 pints
2 metres	R 2 litres	10 metres		$\frac{1}{2}$ hour	6kg	3 miles	

Use one of the numbers from the box to finish each sentence.
Put the letter which is beside the sentence on the line above the
answer. The first one is done for you.

R   A bowl could hold about ____.
O   A school bag could weigh about ____.
H   The time to build a house could be ____.
T   A loaf of bread could weigh about ____.
A   From your shoulder to your fingertip is about ____.
W   Each day Simon is at school about ____.
A   A bed is about ____.
L   A bucket could hold about ____.
U   A walk to keep fit might be about ____ long.
O   From London to Swansea is about ____.
L   A puppy might weigh about ____.
E   A house could be about ____ high.
Y   A programme on T.V. is often about ____.

13. This is a drawing of a church. What shape is

   (a)   the clock

   (b)   a window

   (c)   the spire on the tower

   (d)   the door?

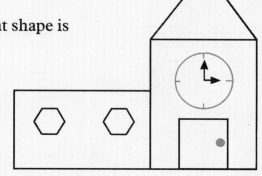

14.

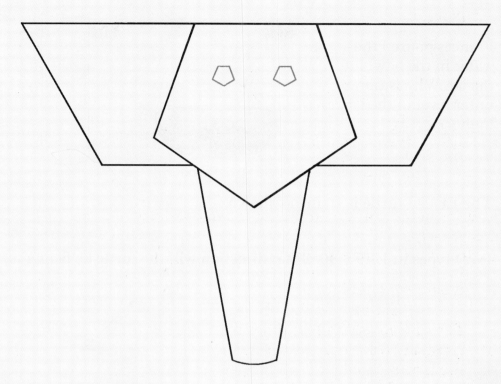

This is a shape picture.

(a)   Make a shape picture from triangles, squares, rectangles, pentagons or hexagons. You may use more than one sort of shape in your picture.

(b)   Write about your picture.

15.   The red shape has been rotated to the grey shape. How many right angles has it been turned through?

(a)   (b)   (c)

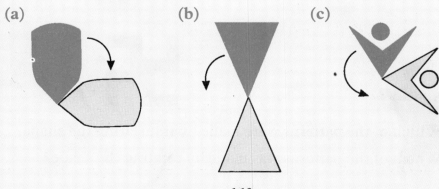

16. Frances poured the water in the bowl into the jar. Why is the water level in the jar higher?

17. The LOGO turtle is facing as shown.

Lucy types in LEFT 90. What direction will the turtle be facing now?

A.   B.   C.   D.

18. The patterns on the right have been made using the shapes on the left.

Shape   Pattern

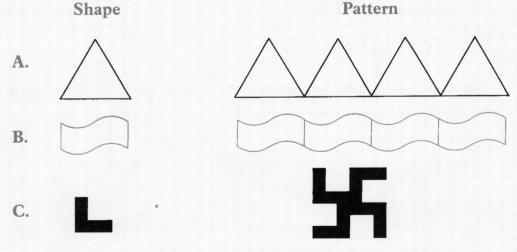

A.

B.

C.

(a) Which of the patterns were made by translating the shape?

(b) Which of the patterns was made by rotating the shape?

Look Around You at . . .

Posting

PRACTICAL 8:1

- Set up your own post office. Make up your own rules about posting. Decide

    — how much it will cost to send letters

    — how much parcels will cost for different weights

    — what times post will be picked up

    — how to send things that could break

    — how you will weigh parcels

    — the shapes of envelopes.

- Make a poster or small book telling people about your postage rules.

MEASURING

DISCUSSION 8:2

● "My cat is 3 hand spans long", said Sam.
"My kitten is as heavy as 20 conkers", said Rachel.
"My dog is 8 little fingers high", said Abel.

What else could Sam, Rachel and Abel have used to measure their animals? Discuss.

● Michael lives 5 streets from school.
Fay lives 184 steps from school.
Justine lives 19 houses from school.

How far do you live from school? Discuss.

● Lilian's bedroom is 4 and a bit strides long.
Lilian drinks 3 glasses of water each day.
Lilian's book is 1 and a bit thumb widths thick.
Lilian's bed is just over 11 of her feet long.

What else could be measured using strides, glasses, thumb widths and feet. Discuss.

● "Measurements always change if a different person does the measuring", says Harry.
"Not always", said Karen. "You have to use a measure that doesn't change."

Discuss what Harry and Karen mean.

PRACTICAL and DISCUSSION 8:3

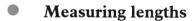

- ### Measuring lengths

  1. Measure the width of your desk using hand spans. Do you get the same answer as the others in your group? Discuss.

  2. Measure the height of your desk using the end of your thumb. Check to see if your group all got the same answer. Discuss.

  3. Measure the width of a window in your classroom using arm length. Did everyone in your group get the same answer? Discuss.

  4. Measure the length of your classroom in strides.

  5. Find other things to measure. Measure them without using a ruler or tape. Discuss your results.

- ### Measuring weight

  You could use conkers, marbles, pens or other small objects for this.

  Pick up something and decide how much it weighs in *conkers* or *marbles*. You might say something like, "This book weighs about the same as 15 marbles". Discuss.

- ### Measuring containers

  You could use beakers, glasses, buckets or cups for this.

  Measure how many containers it takes to fill a sink.

continued . . .

. . . *from previous page*

Inches, feet and yards

1.

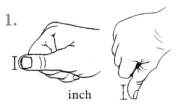   

inch   foot   yard   yard

Many years ago, the yard, the foot and the inch were measured as shown above. These were not always the same as all people did not have the same size thumbs, feet or arms.

Choose some lengths to measure either inside or outside the classroom. Measure some of these using the ways shown above. Did everyone in your group get the same answers? Discuss.

2. How are inches, feet and yards measured now? Why? Discuss.

Using metres, kilograms, pounds

1. Measure the length of your classroom using a tape. Was your answer close to the answers the rest of your group got? Why? Discuss.

2. Measure some other things in metres. Discuss your answers.

3. Find objects you could weigh in kilograms or pounds. Weigh these and discuss your answers.

Finding the best way to measure

Is it best to measure lengths using hand spans, thumb lengths or metres? Why? Discuss.
What is the best way to weigh objects? Discuss.

SMALL MEASURES

DISCUSSION 8:4

●

metre	kilogram	pint	kilometre
litre	pound	ounce	centimetre
feet	inch		

Sally said, "The length of this room would be measured in metres."
Sam said, "A bag of onions is often weighed in pounds."
Make up sentences like Sally's and Sam's for each word in the box. **Discuss** your sentences.

● Ben wanted to find out how heavy his pet mouse was.

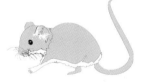

Claire wanted to measure the length of her fingernail.
Tania wanted to know how much water a teaspoon held.

How could Ben, Claire and Tania find out these things?
Discuss.

● Mark wrote, "My garden is about 20m long." What does m mean? **Discuss.**

What is the short way of writing these?

kilogram	litre	kilometre	pound	pint
centimetre	feet	inch		

A ruler is divided into **centimetres**. Each centimetre is divided into **millimetres**. We often write millimetres as **mm**. A pencil is about 8mm wide.

A litre is divided into **millilitres**. Millilitres is often written as **m*l*.** A teaspoon holds about 5 m*l*.

A kilogram is divided into **grams.** We can write this as **g.** We often weigh sugar and flour in grams when we bake a cake.

DISCUSSION 8:5

HARVEST CAKE

3 eggs	400g sugar
155g butter	1 tsp baking powder
2 teaspoons cream of tartar	1 tsp spice
400ml milk	450g flour

What would you use to measure the butter and sugar? What would you use to measure the milk? What would you use to measure the other things you need? Discuss.

What would you do if you only had a 300ml measuring jug to measure the milk with? Discuss.

EXERCISE 8:6

1. What would you use to measure the following? Choose from the pictures below.

   (a) The depth of water in a bath.   (b) The length of a tennis court.

   (c) The width of your thumb.   (d) The weight of 6 sausages.

   (e) The amount of milk in a glass.   (f) The weight of a bag of crisps.

   (g) The distance between two towns.   (h) The amount of medicine to give.

   (i) The weight of 20 potatoes.   (j) The amount of water in a bath.

A. 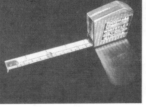   B.    C.

D.    E.    F.

G.    H. 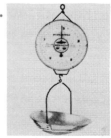   I.

2. Copy each sentence. Choose from the box to fill in the gaps.

cm	kg	km	g	m*l*	*l*	m	mm

(a) The width of this book is about 18 _____.

(b) The height of a classroom could be about 3 _____.

(c) Jason's mother weighed 57 _____.

(d) A slice of cheese weighs about 30 _____.

(e) A mug holds about 250 _____ of water.

(f) A giraffe is about 5 _____ tall.

(g) The largest butterfly ever found was 280 _____ from wing tip to wing tip.

(h) A person drinks about 2 _____ a day.

(i) The length of a pin could be about 30 _____.

(j) The weight of an apple could be about 150 _____.

Review 1 Choose 3 things from your school bag.

(a) Measure the length of each.

(b) Weigh each.

Review 2 What would you use to measure out 100m*l* of milk? Choose from the pictures in **question 1**.

DISCUSSION 8:7

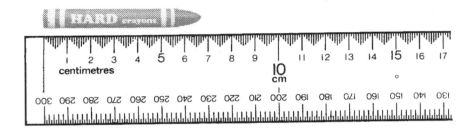

"The crayon is 7cm long to the nearest cm," said Ruth.
"No it's not," said Ben "it's 68mm to the nearest mm."

Discuss these sentences. Who is right?
What does "to the nearest cm" mean? What does "to the nearest mm" mean?
Can we measure the same crayon in cm and mm? **Discuss.**

Measure these lines to the nearest cm. Measure them to the nearest mm. **Discuss** your answers.

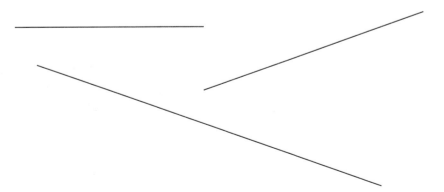

continued . . .

. . . from previous page

Which of these people will be able to tell best, how much water is in the jug? Discuss.

READING SCALES

We read scales to the nearest mark (division).

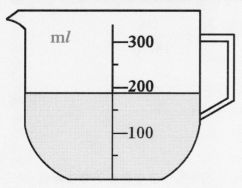

There are 6 marks on this scale. Each one is 50m*l*. Reading to the nearest mark, there are 200m*l* in this jug.

GAME 8:8

HOW CLOSE — a game for a group.

You will need: an object like a pen
a ruler or tape measure
a piece of chalk

Mark a line with chalk about 3m from a wall.

Take turns to:

1. Stand behind the chalk line. Throw the object as close to the wall as you can. **Note:** The object must not hit the wall. If it does, your throw does not count.

2. Measure, to the nearest cm, how far away from the wall the object landed.

    Note: Each person has 3 throws.
    The winner is the person who throws the object closest to the wall. It might be a good idea to use a table like the one below.

Name	1st throw	2nd throw	3rd throw
John	8cm	15cm	7cm
Claire	12cm	—	18cm
Sue			
Salim			
Ted			

EXERCISE 8:9

1. Find the length of these to the nearest mm.

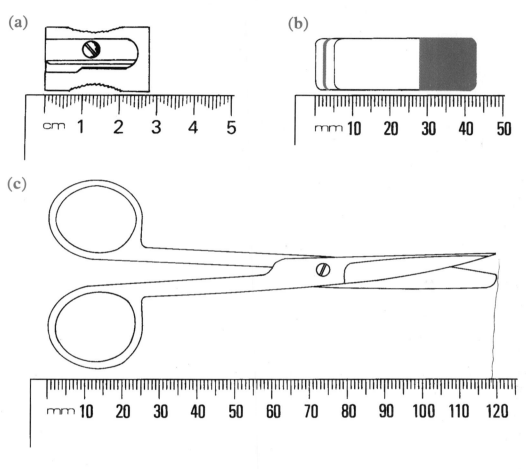

(a)

(b)

(c)

2.

Janet weighed a Christmas present she was sending to a friend. About how much did it weigh?

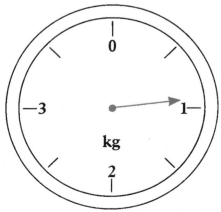

3.

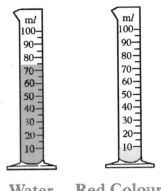

Water   Red Colouring

Andrew had to mix water and red colouring together. How much of each did he mix?

4.   Penny and Tina took the temperature at their houses.

   (a)   What was the temperature at Penny's house?

   (b)   What was the temperature at Tina's house?

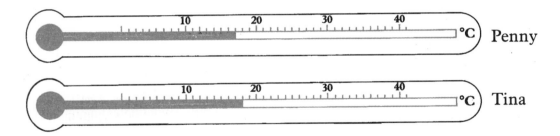

5.   Richard was making fudge. About how much sugar did he use?

6.　Read these scales.

(a) 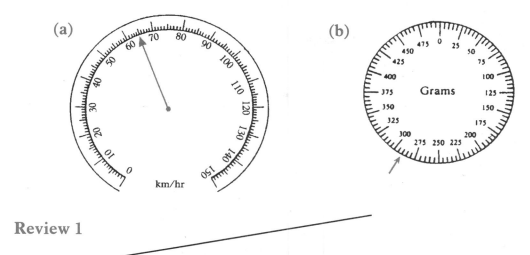 (b)

Review 1

(a)　Measure the length of this line to the nearest mm.

(b)　Measure the length of this line to the nearest cm.

Review 2　Lara was baking a cake. She measured out the butter and sugar first. How much of each did she use?

Butter

Sugar

Review 3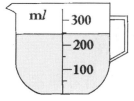

How many m*l* of milk are in this jug?

PRACTICAL 8:10

● Weigh the following coins.

1p   2p   5p   10p   20p   50p   £1

● Cut a 200mm length of cotton. Tie a 500g weight on the end. Keep adding more and more weights until the cotton breaks.

Do this again with a 300mm length and a 400mm length of cotton. Copy and fill in the table below.

Length of cotton	Weight needed to break cotton
200mm 300mm 400mm	

● Make a container that can measure 300m*l*. Put marks at 50m*l*, 100m*l*, 150m*l*, 200m*l*, 250m*l* and 300m*l*. You could use a milk carton, a plastic bottle, a paper cup or you could make your own container.

INVESTIGATIONS 8:11

● INSIDE OUTSIDE

IT HAS BEEN FOUND THAT THE INSIDE OF A CUCUMBER IS 10°C COLDER THAN THE OUTSIDE.

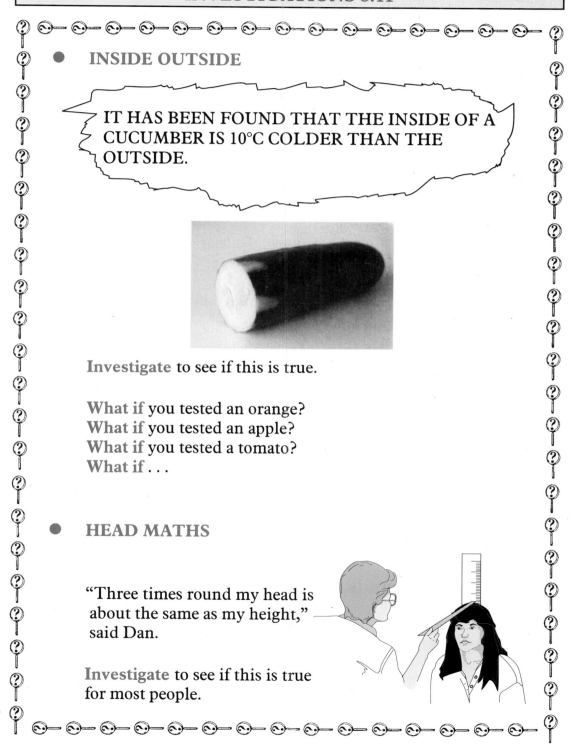

Investigate to see if this is true.

What if you tested an orange?
What if you tested an apple?
What if you tested a tomato?
What if . . .

● HEAD MATHS

"Three times round my head is about the same as my height," said Dan.

Investigate to see if this is true for most people.

ESTIMATING

DISCUSSION 8:12

● Rebecca said, "That window is about $2\frac{1}{2}$ m wide."
"You can't have $\frac{1}{2}$'s in an estimate," said Victoria.

Is Victoria right? Discuss.

● "I drink about one litre of water each day," said Thomas.
"How can you tell?" asked Tina.

What might Thomas say now? Discuss.

● About what size paper do you think you would need to make
     – a poster
     – a birthday card?
Discuss this with your group.

● "A nurse should never estimate amounts," said Christopher.
"Neither should a builder," said Rose.
When could you use an estimate?
When would you not use an estimate?
Discuss.

● **metres, pounds, litres, kilograms, hours, miles, pints**

"A yacht is about 6 metres long", said Tracey.
Make up other sentences using the words above. Discuss your sentences with your group.

PRACTICAL 8:13

● **Estimating Length**

1. Take 3 steps across the room. Mark where you began and ended. Estimate how far this is. Check using a ruler or tape measure.

2. Estimate how tall your teacher is. Check by asking.

3. Estimate what length of paper you would need to put a mural along one wall of your classroom. Check.

4. Estimate the distance from your elbow to the tip of your middle finger. Check using string.

● **Estimating Number**

1. Fill a jar with beans, dried peas, marbles or something else small. Ask the other people in your group to estimate the number of things in the jar.

2. Draw a shape. Fill it with dots. Ask your group to estimate the number of dots.

continued . . .

. . . from previous page

● **Estimating Weight**

1. Find 5 or 6 things that are about the same weight.
   These might be books, a video, a pencil case, a lunch
   box . . .

   Which is heaviest? Which is next
   heaviest? Put them in order.
   Estimate the weight of these
   objects. Check your estimates
   using scales.

2. Weigh a potato or an apple or something like this.
   Estimate how much 5 of these would weigh.
   Check your estimate.

● **Estimating Time**

1. Try and estimate when 1 minute has passed. Ask
   another person in your group to time your estimate.

2. Choose a task to do. You might choose

   — to run to the library and back
   — to sharpen 3 pencils
   — to write down a word 10 times
   — to put some books in alphabetical
     order.

   Estimate how long it will take you to do this task. Ask
   someone in your group to time you.

continued . . .

. . . from previous page

● **Estimating with containers**

Find many different sized containers.

You might find a

- — yoghurt pottle
- — glass
- — test tube
- — plastic bottle
- — teaspoon
- — jug

Choose two of these containers.
Fill the smaller container with water. Tip it into the larger container.
Estimate how many small containers of water it will take to fill the larger one. Check your estimate.

Do this again with two other containers. Use a table like this to write down your estimates and answers.

Small container	Large container	Estimate	Right Answer
teaspoon	yoghurt pottle	25	

EXERCISE 8:14

1. The length of a room could be about

   A. 4m   B. 4cm   C. 50m   D. 50cm.

2. The weight of a baby could be about

   A. 60g

   B. 3g

   C. 3kg

   D. 60kg.

3. The time to eat lunch could be about

   A. 2 hours   B. 15 mins   C. 2 mins   D. 4 hours.

4. Which of these could be about 1m?

   A. a bus   B. a calculator   C. a leg   D. a book

5. Which of these could hold about $1\frac{1}{2}$ litres?

   A. a bath   B. a bucket   C. an eggcup   D. a jug

6. Which of these could take about $\frac{1}{2}$ an hour?

   A. having a bath   B. reading this book   C. making a cup of tea   D. building a fence

7. The distance between two cities could be about

   A. 80km   **B.** 2km   **C.** 300m   **D.** 60cm.

8. The amount of drink in a large glass could be about

   A. $\frac{1}{2}$ litre   **B.** 2 litres   **C.** 50 litres   **D.** 5 litres.

9. Choose from the box to fill in the gaps.

$\frac{1}{2}$ hour	45 kilograms	2 kilometres	2 metres
1 litre	8 kilograms	10 minutes	20 litres

   Jane woke up and jumped out of bed. After a _____ shower she dressed and had breakfast. She put a _____ jug of milk on the table. She walked _____ to school which took her _____. Her school bag was heavy, it weighed _____. Jane herself weighed _____. On the way to school she found a kitten stuck up a tree. It was _____ above her and she couldn't reach it. She frightened the kitten and it jumped into a deep puddle which had about _____ of water in it.

Review

Choose an object from the box that could

(a) weigh about one kilogram
(b) hold about $\frac{1}{2}$ litre
(c) take about an hour to make
(d) be about 2 metres long
(e) weigh about 40kg
(f) be about 20m long.

DISCUSSION 8:15

- **HE LIVES A STONE'S THROW AWAY.**

  How far is a stone's throw? Discuss.

- **I WON'T BE A MOMENT.**

  How long is a moment? Discuss.

- **WALK 10 PACES.**

  How far is a pace? Discuss.

- Think of other sayings like these.
  Estimate the size of the measurements in these. Discuss.

INVESTIGATION 8:16

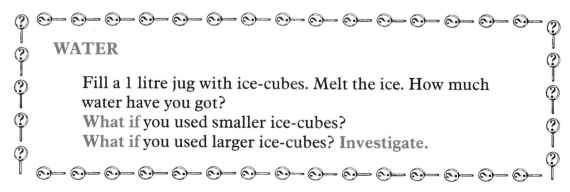

WATER

Fill a 1 litre jug with ice-cubes. Melt the ice. How much water have you got?
What if you used smaller ice-cubes?
What if you used larger ice-cubes? Investigate.

Sometimes when we estimate it is better to overestimate and sometimes it is better to underestimate.

DISCUSSION 8:17

● For each of these, is it better to overestimate or underestimate? Discuss.

The height of a road bridge.

The number of people coming to a party.

Weight of people in a lift.

Maximum Weight 850 kg

The time it takes to drive to a meeting.

Amount of paint needed to paint a room.

The depth of a river you are about to dive into.

● Think of other times it is better to overestimate. Discuss.
Think of other times it is better to underestimate. Discuss.

PUZZLES 8:18

OPTICAL ILLUSIONS

● Which line looks longer? Measure. Were you right?

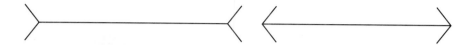

● Which inside square looks bigger? Check.

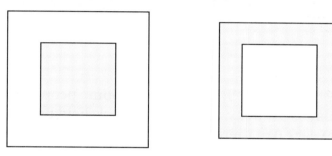

● Which middle circle is larger? Check.

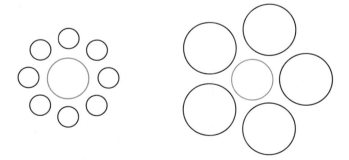

● Which of the red rings looks bigger? Check.

TIME

DISCUSSION 8:19

- We use a **Calendar** to keep track of months and days.
  There are 12 months in a year.
  There are 31 days in January.
  Write down as many facts as you can from a calendar. **Discuss.**

- Friday the 13th is called "Black Friday". Some people believe this day is unlucky. How many Black Fridays will there be this year? Are there always the same number every year? **Discuss.**

- A clock helps us keep track of time in hours and minutes. Draw some different sorts of clocks. **Discuss.**

- "Your father will pick you up at seven thirty," said Lisa's mum. "Do you mean a.m. or p.m?" asked Lisa. What do a.m. and p.m. mean? **Discuss.**

PRACTICAL 8:20

Make your own calendar for a 10-month year. Choose new names for your months, days, seasons . . .

Think about

— how many days will be in a week
— how many days will be in each month
— when will seasons begin and end
— will you have leap years
— how many hours will there be in each day
— will the school day still be the same

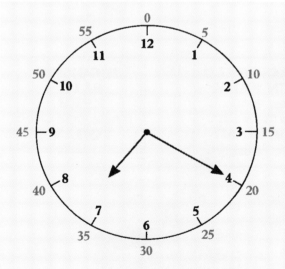

This clock has two hands. The short hand tells us the hour and the long hand tells us the minutes.

For the hour hand each mark is one hour.

For the minute hand each mark is 5 minutes. These are shown in red.

This clock reads 20 minutes past 7. We write this as 7:20.

Times before noon have a.m. beside them. Times after noon have p.m. beside them.

7:45 at night is 7:45 p.m.   8:20 in the morning is 8:20 a.m.

EXERCISE 8:21

1. How many minutes are there in an hour?

2. Are these a.m. or p.m. times?

    (a) Emma gets up at 7:15.

    (b) Sharon goes to bed at 8:00.

    (c) Brenda catches the bus home
         from school at 4:05.

    (d) Kai eats lunch at 12:45.

    (e) Hannah's race begins at 11:25.

3. Would you put a.m. or p.m. on these signs?

    (a) **DAILY**
    7:30 ....
    The Kent
    Choir
    LIVE IN
    CONCERT

    (b) **BLACKFIELD**
    FUN PARK
    Open 9:00 ....
    to 7:00 ....
    Fun for all
    the family

    (c) **BIGGEST**
    SALE
    EVER
    Ends 5:30 ....
    TODAY

4.

						M	
12:25	10:10	1:15		9:30	6:00	4:20	2:45

5:50	11:35	2:40	3:55	8:05

Copy the box. Find the time on each of the clocks below. Put the letter beside the clock on the line above the answer. The first one is done for you. The time is 4:20 so **M** is put on the line above 4:20.

M  **L**  **W**  **S**

I 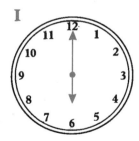 **O**  **I**  **E**

T 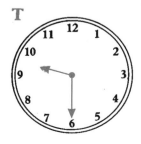 **F** 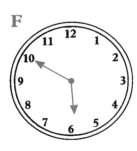 **H** 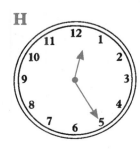 **E**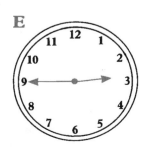

5.

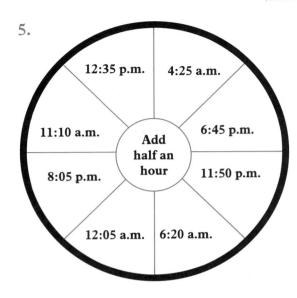

Add half an hour to each time on the wheel. Begin at 4:25 a.m.

Review 1   Write down what you were doing yesterday at these times.

(a) 7.50 a.m.   (b) 6.30 p.m.   (c) 12.45 p.m.

(d) 2.20 p.m.   (e) 3.30 p.m.

Review 2   What time is shown on these clocks?

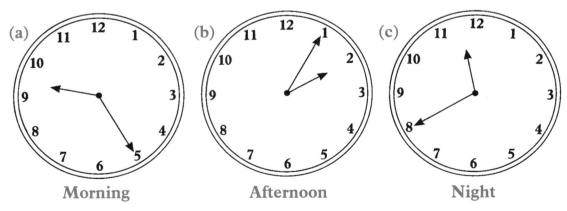

(a) Morning   (b) Afternoon   (c) Night

(d)   What would the time be half an hour after the time shown on the clock in (c)?

DISCUSSION 8:22

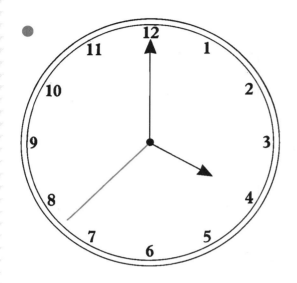

Some clocks and watches have a third hand. What does this tell us? **Discuss**.

● What is a stopwatch? **Discuss**. Which of these would you use a stopwatch for? **Discuss**.

— to time a 100m running race

— to time how long it takes to drive from London to Glasgow

— to time a marathon

— to time a swimming race

● When else might we use a stopwatch? **Discuss**.

There are 60 seconds in one minute. A stopwatch measures time in seconds.

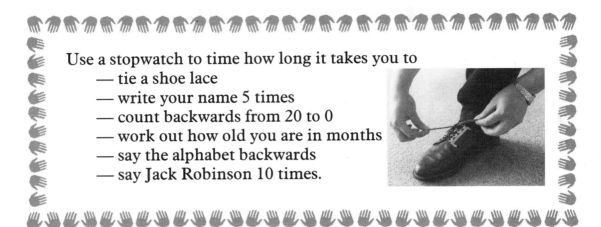

PRACTICAL 8:23

Use a stopwatch to time how long it takes you to
— tie a shoe lace
— write your name 5 times
— count backwards from 20 to 0
— work out how old you are in months
— say the alphabet backwards
— say Jack Robinson 10 times.

24-HOUR TIME

Twenty past eight could be in the morning or at night. The 24-hour clock numbers the hours after midday as 13, 14, 15, . . .

MORNING

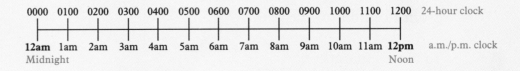

AFTERNOON AND EVENING

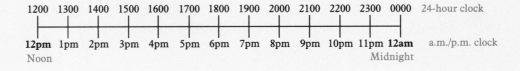

3:20 p.m. is written as 1520 hours on a 24-hour clock. We say this as "fifteen twenty hours." Twenty-four-hour clock times always have 4 digits. 8:20 a.m. is written as 0820.

Worked Example   Bhupinder got up at 6:45 a.m. and went to bed at 8:10 p.m. Write these as 24-hour clock times.

Answer   6:45a.m. is in the morning. It is written as 0645 hours. 8:10 p.m. is in the evening. 8 p.m. is 2000 hours so 8:10 p.m. is 2010 hours.

EXERCISE 8:24

1. Write these as 24-hour clock times.

  (a) 4 a.m.   (b) 9 a.m.   (c) 10 p.m.   (d) 2 p.m.

  (e) 12 a.m.   (f) 1 a.m.   (g) 7 p.m.   (h) 8:30 p.m.

  (i) 4:20 a.m.   (j) 6:05 p.m.   (k) 11:55 p.m.   (l) 12:37 a.m.

  (m) twenty past four in the afternoon

  (n) 10 minutes to eight at night

  (o) 15 minutes to 5 in the morning

  (p) 20 minutes to two in the afternoon

2. The disco at Rex's school started at 7:00 p.m. and ended at 10:15 p.m. Write these as 24-hour clock times.

3. Jan's baby sister was born at 3:25 a.m. What time is this on the 24-hour clock?

4. Write these as a.m. or p.m. times.

   (a) 0400   (b) 2100   (c) 0800   (d) 1400   (e) 1800

   (f) 0745   (g) 0905   (h) 1115   (i) 0010   (j) 1420

   (k) 2350   (l) 1935   (m) 1640   (n) 0410   (o) 0050

5. Robert missed the train by 10 minutes. He got to the station at 8:25 a.m. Write down, in 24-hour clock time, the time the train left.

6.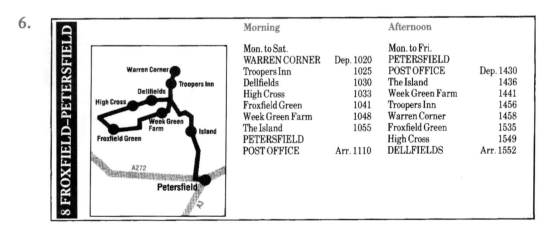

	Morning		Afternoon	
	Mon. to Sat.		Mon. to Fri.	
WARREN CORNER	Dep. 1020		PETERSFIELD	
Troopers Inn	1025		POST OFFICE	Dep. 1430
Dellfields	1030		The Island	1436
High Cross	1033		Week Green Farm	1441
Froxfield Green	1041		Troopers Inn	1456
Week Green Farm	1048		Warren Corner	1458
The Island	1055		Froxfield Green	1535
PETERSFIELD			High Cross	1549
POST OFFICE	Arr. 1110		DELLFIELDS	Arr. 1552

This is a Postbus timetable.

(a) In a.m./p.m. time, when does the bus leave High Cross in the morning?

(b) In a.m./p.m. time, when in the afternoon does the bus reach Dellfields?

(c) In a.m./p.m. time, when in the morning does the bus reach Petersfield Post Office?

Review 1 Write these as 24-hour clock times.

(a) 3:20 p.m. (b) 10:05 a.m. (c) 12:10 a.m.

(d) 5 minutes to 6 at night

Review 2 This gives the times for the "Edenbridge Town Service".

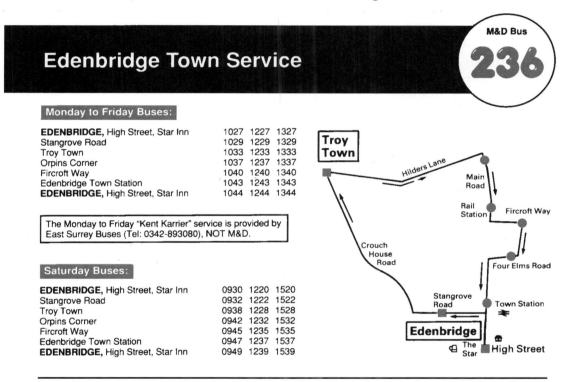

(a) In a.m./p.m. time, what time do buses leave Fircroft Way on Monday?

(b) In a.m./p.m. time, what time do buses leave Edenbridge, High Street on Saturday?

Review 3 Sandy had to take the cat to the vet at 1620. What time is this in a.m./p.m. time?

GAME 8:25

GUESS MY TIME - a game for a group.

You will need: Paper and pencil

Choose a leader.
The leader writes down a time. This can be written as a.m./p.m.
time or 24-hour clock time.
Others in the group ask 15 questions to try and guess the time.
The leader may only say **yes** or **no**.

Here is an example of a game played by Ken, Amy, Fay and Brad.
Ken thought of the time 1515.

Amy:	Is it a 24-hour clock time?
Ken:	Yes.
Fay:	Is it a time before noon?
Ken:	No.
Brad:	Is it between 1800 and midnight?
Ken:	No.
Fay:	Has it got a 3, 4 or 5 as its second digit?
Ken:	Yes.
Amy:	Is it between 1400 and 1500?
Ken:	No.
Brad:	Is it between 1500 and 1600?
Ken:	Yes.
Fay:	Is it between 1500 and 1530?
Ken:	Yes.
Amy:	Is it 1515?
Ken:	Yes.

Amy is the new leader.

WORK THIS OUT

1. Senga wants to catch the 1400 bus to Bishop's Waltham. She thinks her watch is 5 minutes slow but it is really 10 minutes fast. Rod wants to catch the same bus. Rod's watch is 10 minutes slow, but he thinks it is 10 minutes fast. Who will miss the bus?

2. You have a jug which you know holds 3 litres and one which you know holds 2 litres. How could you use these to measure out
   — 5 litres
   — 1 litres
   — 7 litres?

Look Around You at . . .

Art

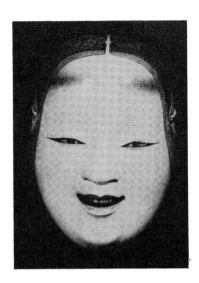

DISCUSSION 9:1

●   "Artists often use symmetry," said Tessa.

What does *symmetry* mean? **Discuss.**

●   "I like symmetrical designs better than ones which aren't symmetrical," said Sam.

Which do you like? **Discuss.**

●   Do some types of art, like Japanese or Islamic art, have more symmetry than art from other places? Find out as much as you can. **Discuss** what you found with your group or class.

LINES of SYMMETRY

A shape has **symmetry** if it can be folded so that one half fits onto the other half.

Example 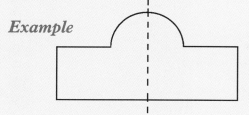 If this shape was folded along the dotted line, the two halves would fit on top of one another. The dotted line is a **line of symmetry**.

PRACTICAL 9:2

● Take a sheet of paper.

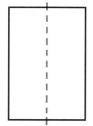  

Fold it in half. Draw a shape. Cut it out. Open it out.

Make some more shapes this way.

● Take 6 sheets of paper. Fold each in half. Draw the lines shown in red and cut along them. What shapes have you made?

continued . . .

. . . from previous page

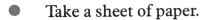

● Take a sheet of paper.

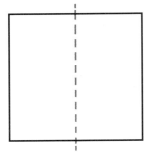

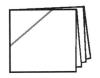

Fold it in half.   Fold in half again.

Draw the line shown in red. Cut along it. Guess what shape you will get. Open the paper out to see.

● Work out how to make these shapes using folded paper.

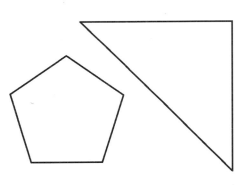

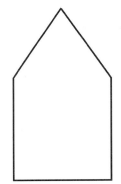

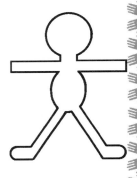

● Take a sheet of paper.

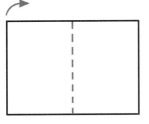

Fold in half again.

Fold it in half.   Fold in half again.

continued . . .

. . . from previous page

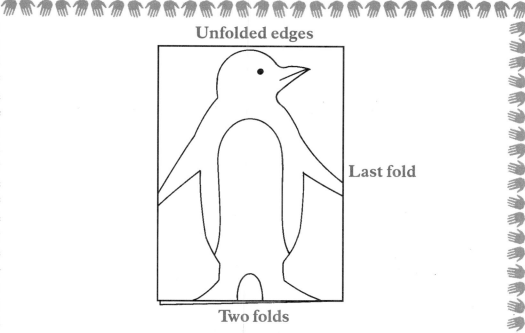

Unfolded edges

Last fold

Two folds

Draw the picture above onto your folded paper.
Cut the penguin out.
This is what it looks like when you open it out.

Give each penguin a face and a suit.

Make up a design of your own using folded paper.

DISCUSSION 9:3

● These shapes are not symmetrical. What would you need to add to make each symmetrical? **Discuss.**
Note: the dotted line is a line of symmetry.

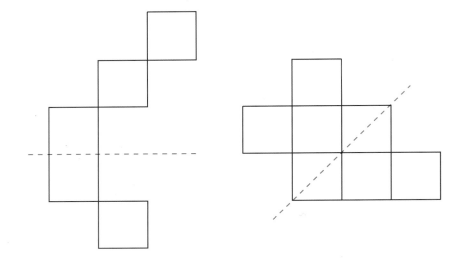

● Often shapes and pictures will be symmetrical in some parts but not others. We can also find many *almost* symmetrical shapes in nature. Leaves and flowers are good examples. Look at the pictures below and on the next page. **Discuss** the symmetry of each.

continued . . .

. . . from previous page

PRACTICAL AND DISCUSSION 9:4

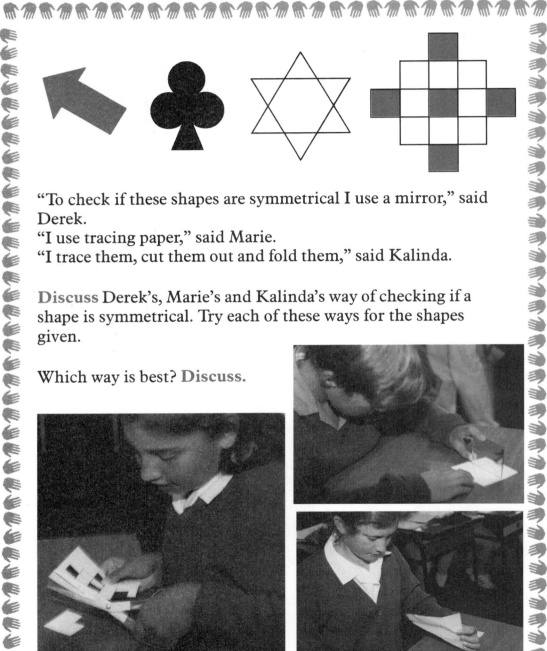

"To check if these shapes are symmetrical I use a mirror," said Derek.

"I use tracing paper," said Marie.

"I trace them, cut them out and fold them," said Kalinda.

Discuss Derek's, Marie's and Kalinda's way of checking if a shape is symmetrical. Try each of these ways for the shapes given.

Which way is best? **Discuss.**

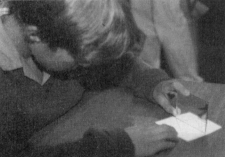

PRACTICAL 9:5

Use **LOGO** on your computer.

In LOGO   PU means PEN UP. The turtle will not leave a line when it moves.

PD means PEN DOWN. Use it when you want to draw again.

HOME means the turtle will go back to where it started.

The following will draw one half of a T.

```
RIGHT 90
FORWARD 20
LEFT 90
FORWARD 150
RIGHT 90
FORWARD 60
LEFT 90
FORWARD 40
LEFT 90
FORWARD 80
PU
HOME
```

Draw the other half of the T.

Start as follows

```
PD
LEFT 90
FORWARD 20
 . . .
 . . .
```

EXERCISE 9:6

1.

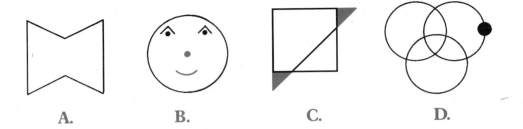

A.   B.   C.   D.

Which of these shapes has   (a)   just one line of symmetry

(b)   more than one line of symmetry

(c)   no lines of symmetry?

2.   Trace the shapes from **question 1** that are symmetrical.
Draw the lines of symmetry on these.

3.   Match these halves to get symmetrical faces.

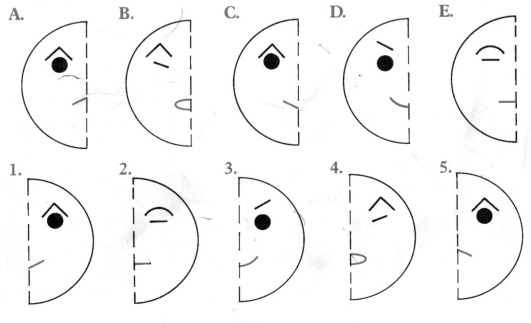

4.   Which of these shapes are symmetrical?

(a)

(b)

(c)

(d)

(e)

`(f)

(g)

(h)

(i)

5. Draw a shape which has (a) one line of symmetry

(b) two lines of symmetry.

6. Copy this shape. Add one square to make it symmetrical.

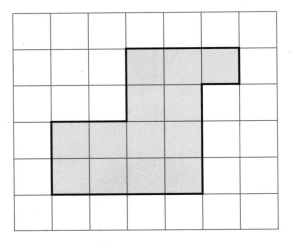

7. How many lines of symmetry has each shape got? Copy each shape and draw the lines of symmetry.

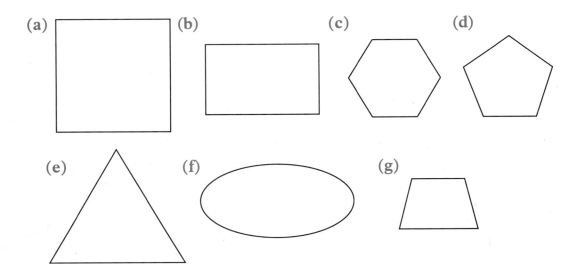

(a)   (b)   (c)   (d)

(e)   (f)   (g)

Review 1

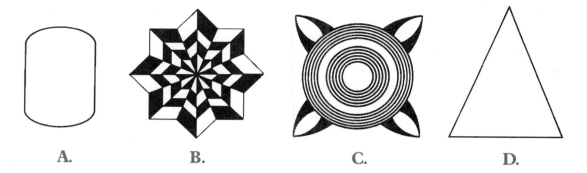

A.   B.   C.   D.

Which of these shapes has (a) just one line of symmetry

(b) no lines of symmetry

(c) more than one line of symmetry?

Review 2 Match these halves to get symmetrical shapes.

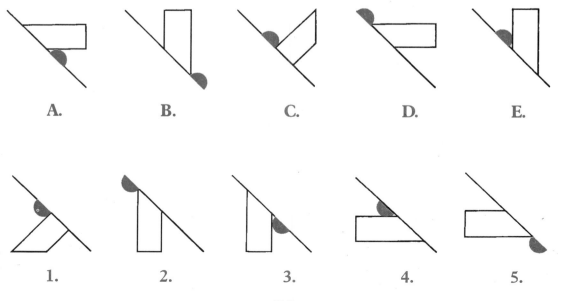

A.   B.   C.   D.   E.

1.   2.   3.   4.   5.

INVESTIGATIONS 9:7

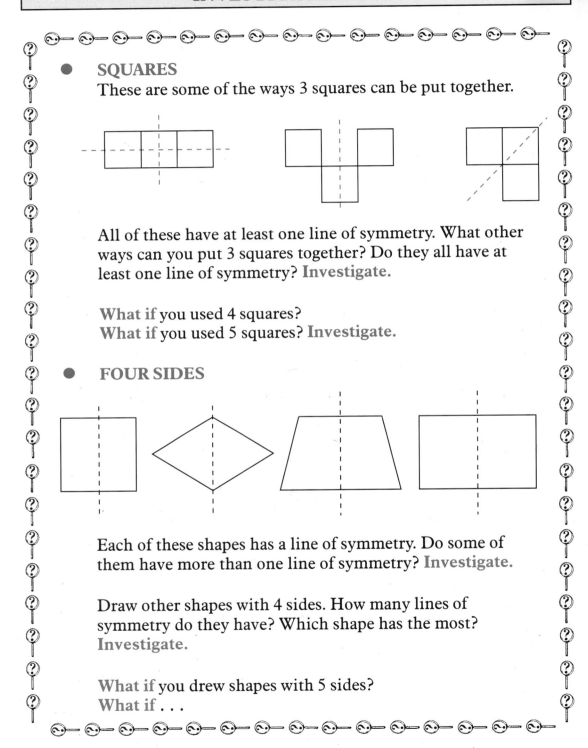

- **SQUARES**

  These are some of the ways 3 squares can be put together.

  All of these have at least one line of symmetry. What other ways can you put 3 squares together? Do they all have at least one line of symmetry? **Investigate.**

  What if you used 4 squares?
  What if you used 5 squares? **Investigate.**

- **FOUR SIDES**

  Each of these shapes has a line of symmetry. Do some of them have more than one line of symmetry? **Investigate.**

  Draw other shapes with 4 sides. How many lines of symmetry do they have? Which shape has the most? **Investigate.**

  What if you drew shapes with 5 sides?
  What if . . .

PRACTICAL 9:8

Some Islamic art is made by using a symmetrical design over and over again.

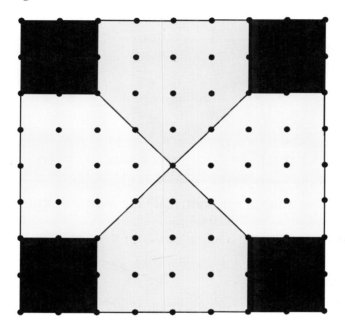

On dotty paper draw a symmetrical design like the one shown at the top. Use this design to make your own Islamic pattern.

PLANES of SYMMETRY

DISCUSSION 9:9

● "We can't trace around a tin or a toblerone box and fold it in half," said Blair "but I think it is symmetrical."

Are these shapes symmetrical? How do you know? Discuss.

●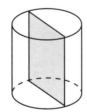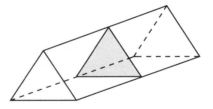

What is the shaded part called? Discuss.

●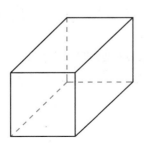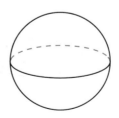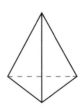

How can we tell if these shapes are symmetrical? Discuss.
Can you draw a shaded part that cuts the shape in half?
Discuss.

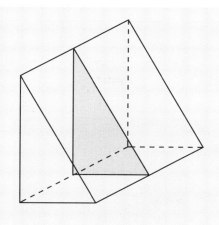

This shape is symmetrical.
The shaded part is called a **plane of symmetry**. A plane of symmetry cuts a solid shape into two equal parts.

PRACTICAL 9:10

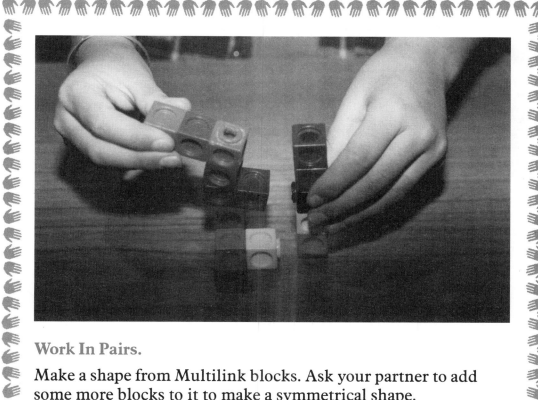

Work In Pairs.

Make a shape from Multilink blocks. Ask your partner to add some more blocks to it to make a symmetrical shape.

Make some more shapes to give to your partner.

EXERCISE 9:11

1. Which of these shapes are symmetrical?

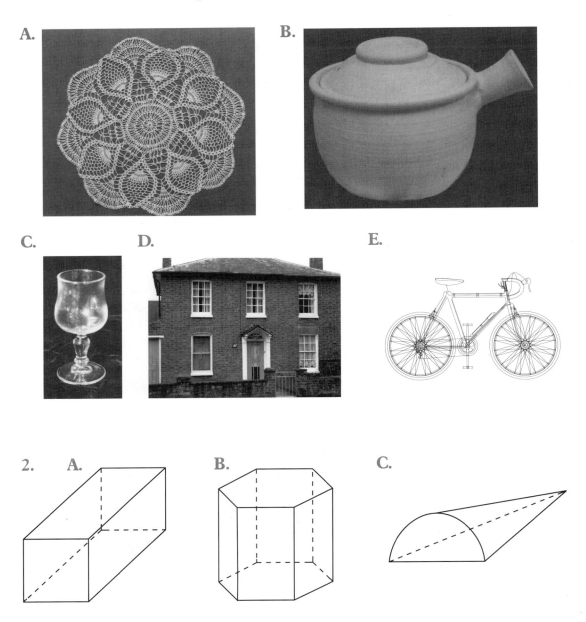

A.

B.

C.

D.

E.

2. A.

B.

C.

Which shapes have (a) one plane of symmetry

(b) more than one plane of symmetry?

3.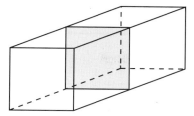

A plane of symmetry is shaded.
Trace this shape and shade another
plane of symmetry.

Review 1 Look around you. Name things which have

    (a) one plane of symmetry

    (b) more than one plane of symmetry

    (c) no planes of symmetry.

Review 2 Which of these shapes have

    (a) one plane of symmetry

    (b) more than one plane of symmetry

    (c) no planes of symmetry?

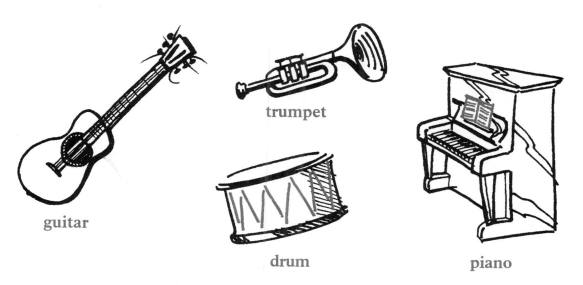

trumpet

guitar

drum

piano

PRACTICAL 9:12

This is a building in India. It is symmetrical.

This photo has some examples of symmetry.

continued . . .

. . . from previous page

Choose a subject like buildings or photos and find as many examples of symmetry as you can. Make a poster or book or give a talk on what you found.
Here are some other ideas.

> Nature (leaves, flowers)
> P.E.
> Cakes
> Sport (ballet, football . . .)
> Marching teams
> Animals
> Cards
> Logos
> Traffic Signs

● Make something which is symmetrical and show it to your class. You could make

— a pencil case

— a model robot

— a decorated cake

— a Christmas tree decoration.

WORK THIS OUT

Draw these shapes on squared paper. Put them together to make a symmetrical shape.
There is more than one way for some of them.

1.

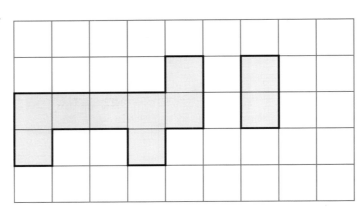

(1 way)

2.

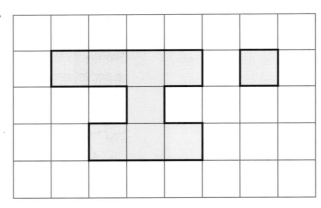

(2 ways)

3.

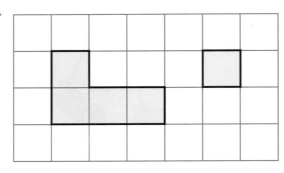

(3 ways)

4.

(4 ways)

Look Around You at . . .

Parties

PRACTICAL 10:1

- Think of many different sorts of parties. Choose one of these. Draw or write about the shapes that you might find at this party. Think about
  - food
  - what people might wear
  - what people watch or listen to or play . . .

  Make a poster, collage or story about party shapes.

- You have been asked to make the cake for this party. Draw pictures of the cake you would make. Make sure you show how you would decorate it.

3. This is a shape sorting machine.

Which shapes in **question 2** would end up in

(a) box 1   (b) box 2   (c) box 3   (d) box 4?

4.

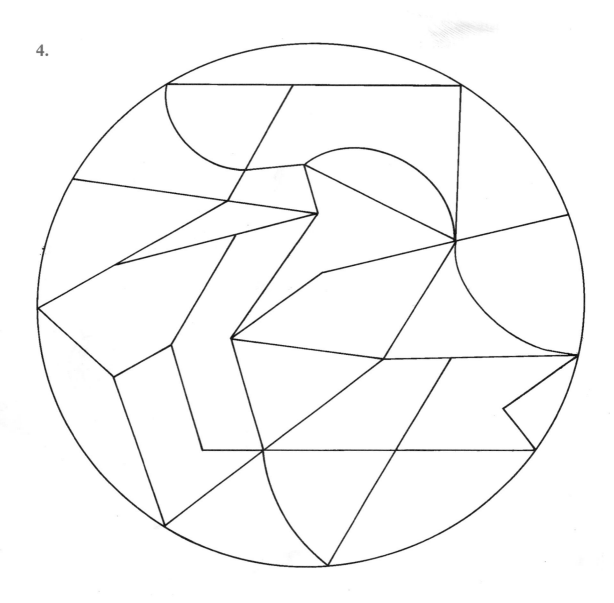

Trace this into your book.

Shade all the shapes that have one or more curved edges.

Shade all the shapes which have 5 sides.

You will have something white and beautiful left. What is it?

5. Kelly sorted some shapes into two groups.

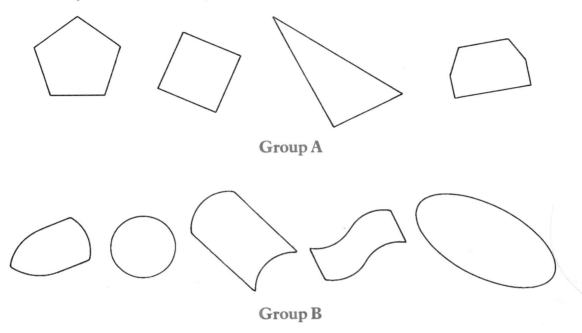

Group A

Group B

Which group would each of these shapes be in?
How can you tell?

(a)   **(b)**   **(c)**   **(d)**

6. Copy the table and fill it in.

SHAPE	Number of equal sides	Number of straight sides	Number of curved sides
▢			
◠			
◯			
△			
⬠			
⬡			

7. Copy the table and fill it in.

SHAPE	Number of faces	Number of edges	Number of vertices
(cuboid)			
(oblique prism)			
(pyramid)			
(L-shaped prism)			

8. Sort the shapes in the table in **question 6** into 2 groups. Explain how you sorted them.

9. Sort the shapes in the table in **question 7** into 2 groups. Explain how you sorted them.

10. Draw a shape which has 5 sides and one right angle.

11. Draw a shape which has no vertices.

Review 1

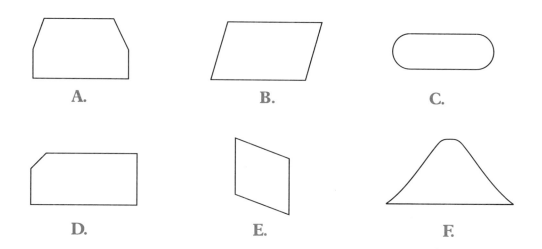

A.

B.

C.

D.

E.

F.

Which of these shapes have (a) more than 4 sides

(b) a curved side

(c) just 2 right angles

(d) straight and curved sides

(e) symmetry?

Review 2

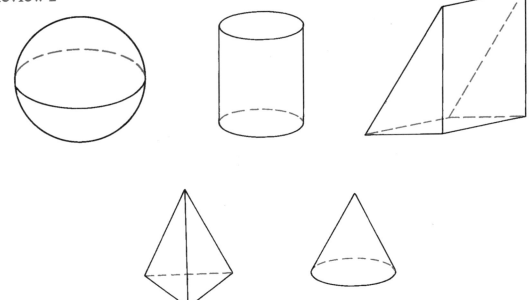

These shapes were sorted into 3 groups.
Group 1 has shapes with no vertices.
Group 2 has shapes with no curved surfaces.
Group 3 has shapes with just one vertex.

Which shapes are in   (a)   group 1

                   (b)   group 2

                   (c)   group 3?

(d)   Which group would this shape be in? How do you know?

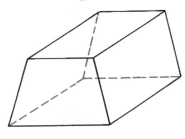

GAME 10:6

GUESS MY SHAPE – a game for 2 to 4 players

Decide who will start.
This player thinks of a shape and tells the rest of the group about it.

Example

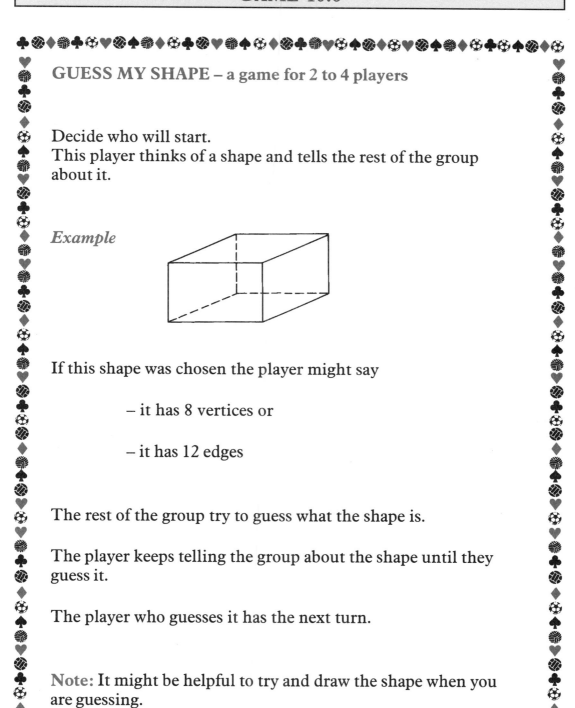

If this shape was chosen the player might say

– it has 8 vertices or

– it has 12 edges

The rest of the group try to guess what the shape is.

The player keeps telling the group about the shape until they guess it.

The player who guesses it has the next turn.

Note: It might be helpful to try and draw the shape when you are guessing.

PRACTICAL 10:7

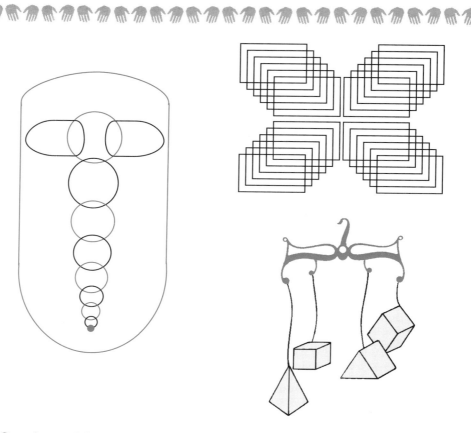

Carolyn said, "I am going to make a mobile from shapes that have no curved surfaces."

Rashid said, "I'm going to make a wallpaper pattern from shapes that have right angles."

George said, "I'm going to make a bookmark with shapes that have curved sides."

Jacky said, "I'm going to make a wall hanging from shapes that are symmetrical."

Make a mobile or wallpaper pattern or bookmark or wall hanging. Choose a group of shapes like Carolyn, Rashid, George and Jacky did.

Colour your shapes.

INVESTIGATIONS 10:8

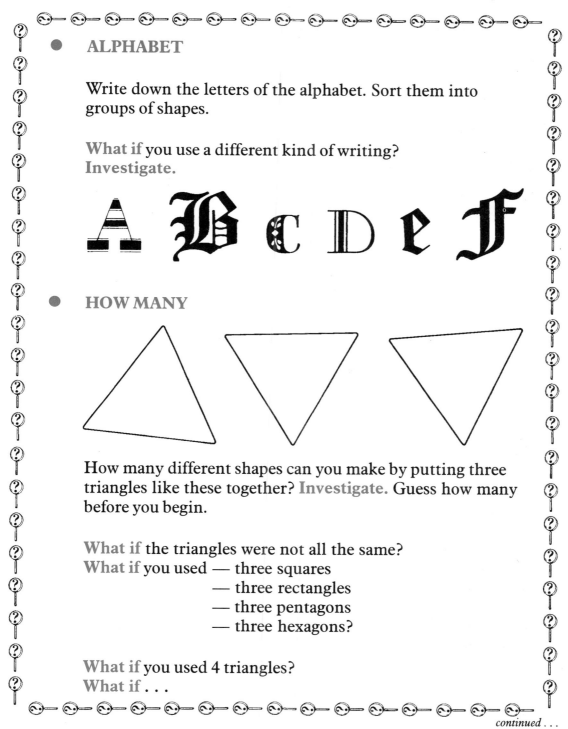

● **ALPHABET**

Write down the letters of the alphabet. Sort them into groups of shapes.

What if you use a different kind of writing? **Investigate.**

● **HOW MANY**

How many different shapes can you make by putting three triangles like these together? **Investigate.** Guess how many before you begin.

What if the triangles were not all the same?
What if you used — three squares
— three rectangles
— three pentagons
— three hexagons?

What if you used 4 triangles?
What if . . .

continued . . .

. . . from previous page

● **SIGNS**

Investigate the shape of signs. You may like to make a table, a poster or give a talk about what you find.

MAKING PATTERNS with SHAPES

DISCUSSION 10:9

- Patterns can be made in many different ways.
  One way is to start with a design and keep sliding it along.

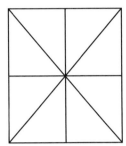 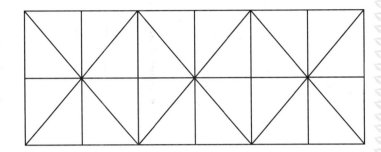

Think of other ways patterns can be made. **Discuss**.

- Sometimes patterns are made by sliding (translating) or turning (rotating) shapes or by making symmetrical shapes. How have these patterns been made? **Discuss**.

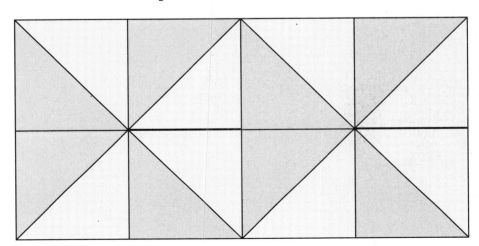

continued . . .

. . . from previous page

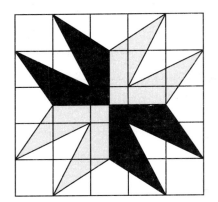
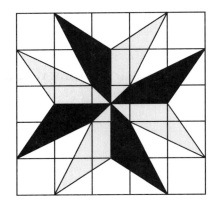

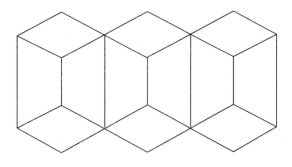

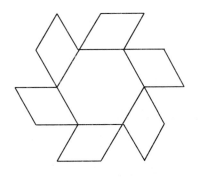
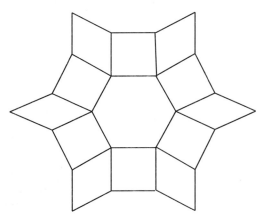

PRACTICAL 10:10

1. Draw a triangle like the one below. Make a pattern by
   sliding it, turning it or making symmetrical shapes with it.
   Colour your pattern using just two colours.

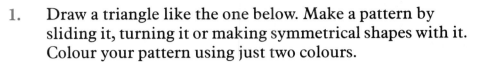

2. Do Number 1. again using one of these shapes.

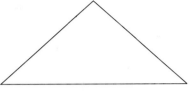

3. Do Number 1. again using any two shapes you like.

4. These two triangle designs are the same but they are
   coloured differently.

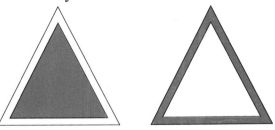

   Make a pattern by sliding or turning them or making
   symmetrical shapes with them. You could cut each in half
   and make patterns with the halves.

continued . . .

. . . from previous page

5. Do Number 4. again starting with two other shapes that are coloured differently.

6. People all around the world make patterns by sliding and turning designs or making them symmetrical.
Some make baskets, some make cloth, some make mats, some make other things. Some of these people are

> Babuka people of Central Africa
> Yoruba people of West Africa
> Islamic people
> Maori people of New Zealand
> Samoan people
> American Indians
> Assante people of Ghana
> Mende people of West Africa

Find out about patterns made by people from another country. What do they make with these patterns? How are the patterns made? Make a poster or book about what you find out.

7. Shapes can be made to look solid by sliding them along.

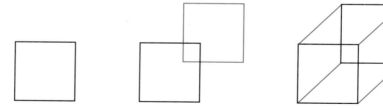

Draw a square.　　Slide it along.　　Join the matching corners.

Make some other solid shapes this way.

WORK THIS OUT

1. I am two shapes put together.
   I have 9 faces and 9 vertices.
   I have 16 edges.
   Whole I have no name.
   Split I have two.
   Draw me.

2. Take away 6 matches to leave 3 squares.

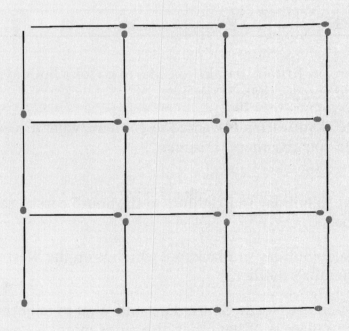

Look Around You at . . .

Holidays

DISCUSSION AND PRACTICAL 11:1

- Where, in Britain, would you like to go for a holiday? How would you get there? Discuss.

  If one of your friends wanted to go there, what directions would you give them? Discuss.

- "I like to holiday in Brighton on the South coast," said Jenufa.

  "I like to holiday in Blackpool which is on the West coast," said Jenufa's mother.

  We often use North, South, East and West to tell others where a place is. What other directions might we use? Discuss.

- Make a booklet about a place you would like to go for a holiday. Put pictures in and give directions on how to get there.

CLOCKWISE and ANTICLOCKWISE

DISCUSSION 11:2

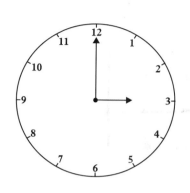

Copy this clock. Show, with an arrow, which way the hands move. What do we call this direction? Discuss.

A fly walked the shortest way from 4 around the outside to 12. We can say the fly is moving _____. What word could fill the gap? Discuss.

"The sun moves clockwise across the sky," said Beverley. Is this true? Discuss.

When you turn left and move round in a circle, are you moving clockwise or anticlockwise? Discuss.

This arrow shows a move in a clockwise direction. Clockwise is the direction in which the hands of a clock move.

This arrow shows a move in an anticlockwise direction. This is the opposite direction to clockwise.

GAME 11:3

RAINBOW – a game for 2 players.

You will need: 2 different coloured counters
a cube (or die)
the board on the next page

First Put A1, A2, A3, C1, C2, C3 on the six faces of a cube.
A1 means move anticlockwise 1 square.
C2 means move clockwise 2 squares

and so on

The game

1. Each player puts a counter on one of the START squares on the board on the next page.

2. Decide who starts.

3. Take turns to toss the cube. Move clockwise or anticlockwise, the number of squares given on the cube.

The winner is the first person to reach the pot of gold at the end of the rainbow.

Note: You must get the EXACT number needed to reach the pot of gold.
If you toss A3 and you need A2 to reach the pot of gold then you can't move.

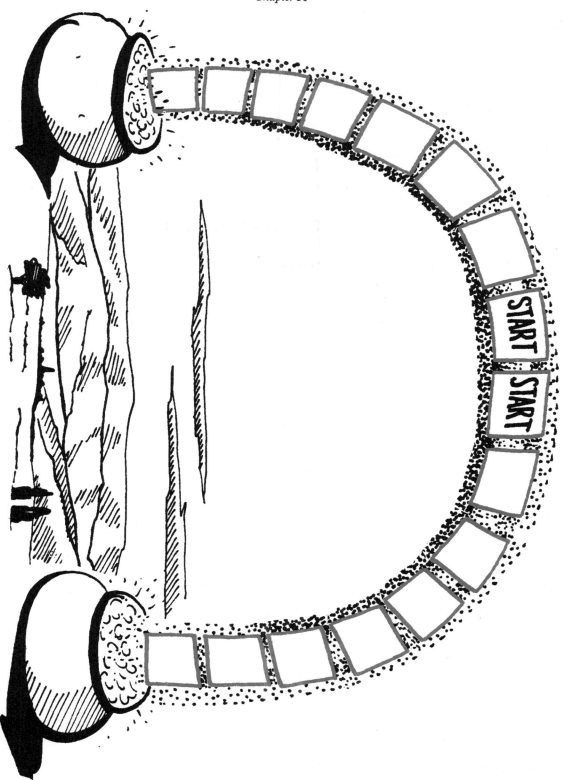

COMPASS DIRECTIONS

DISCUSSION 11:4

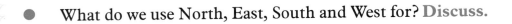

- Birds fly South in winter.
  It is cold at the North Pole.
  Southend-On-Sea is on the East Coast of England.
  Ireland is to the West of Wales.

  Make up some more sentences which
  have the words North, East, West and
  South. What do these words mean?
  Discuss.

- What do we use North, East, South and West for? Discuss.

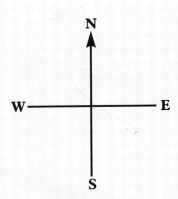

N is North
E is East
S is South
W is West

North, East, South and West are called compass directions.

Worked Example

(a) From the park Matthew walked East. At the corner he turned North and walked to his friend's house. Whose house did Matthew go to?

(b) What direction is Jon's house from Jo's house?

Answer (a)

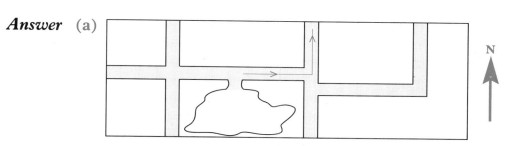

Matthew walked to Sue's house.

(b) North

EXERCISE 11:5

1.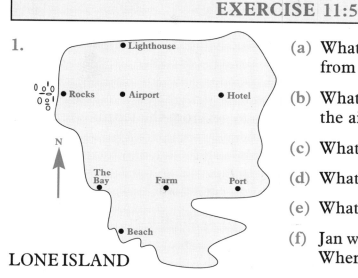

LONE ISLAND

(a) What direction is the airport from the lighthouse?

(b) What direction is the hotel from the airport?

(c) What is North of the airport?

(d) What is East of the farm?

(e) What is West of the airport?

(f) Jan walked West from the farm. Where did she walk to?

2. This is camp Wonderland.

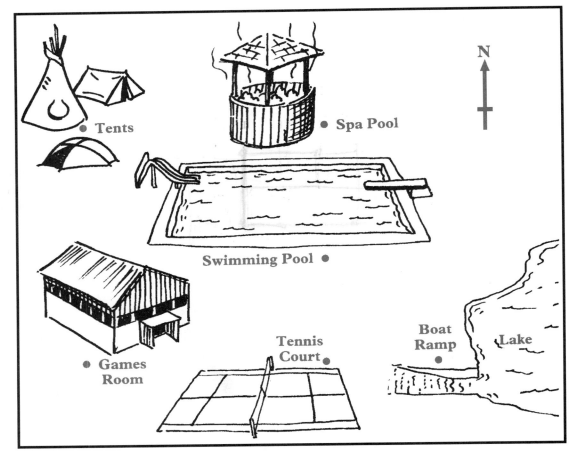

(a) What direction is the Spa pool from the tennis court?

(b) What is South of the tents?

(c) In which direction do you go to get from the tennis court to the boat ramp?

(d) What is North of the tennis court?

(e) What direction is the spa pool from the tents?

(f) What is West of the Boat Ramp?

3. Which direction would you be facing after doing this?

   1. Face West.

   2. Turn clockwise through 1 right angle.

   3. Walk 6 steps forward.

   4. Turn anticlockwise through 2 right angles.

4.

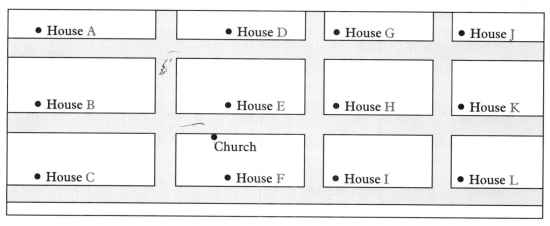

Follow these directions. At each corner change direction.
Start at the Church. Go West, then North, then East, then South, then East, then North, then West. What is the last house you passed?

5.

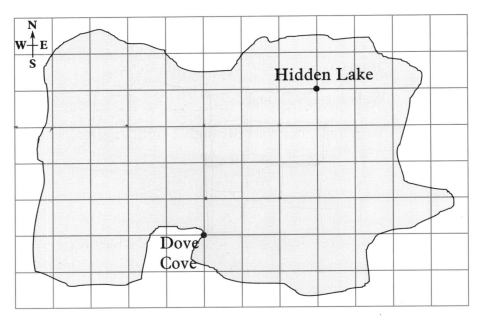

On this diagram, the length of each square is 50m.

Four people land at this island at Dove Cove.
They each set off in search of Hidden Lake.
The routes they follow are given below.

Which of these people find Hidden Lake?

Andrea 50m North, then 200m East, then 100m North, then 350m West, then 50m North, then 200m East, then 200m South, then 50m West.

Adam 150m North, then 50m East, then 50m North, then 150m East, then 200m South, then 200m West.

Keith 150m East, then 150m North, then 150m West, then 150m South, then 100m North, then 100m East, then 100m North, then 100m West, then 200m South.

Karen 50m East, then 50m North, then 50m East, then 50m North, then 50m East, then 50m North, then 50m West, then 50m North, then 50m East, then 150m West, then 200m South.

Review 1

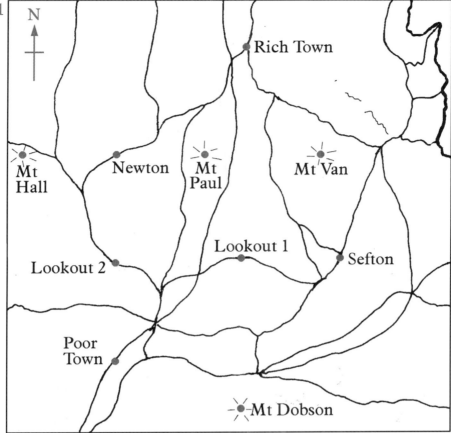

(a) What is North of Lookout 2?

(b) What is South of Lookout 1?

(c) What direction is Mt. Hall from Mt. Van?

(d) What is West of Mt. Paul?

(e) What is East of Lookout 2?

Review 2 Jolene is facing East. She then

1. turns anticlockwise through a half turn

2. walks 8 steps forward

3. turns clockwise through 3 right angles.

What direction is she facing now?

PUZZLE 11:6

PATHS

Copy this.

<u>1</u>   <u>2</u> <u>3</u> <u>4</u> <u>5</u>   <u>6</u> <u>7</u> <u>8</u>   <u>9</u> <u>10</u> <u>11</u> <u>12</u>   <u>13</u> <u>14</u> <u>15</u>   <u>16</u> <u>17</u> <u>18</u> <u>19</u>

I

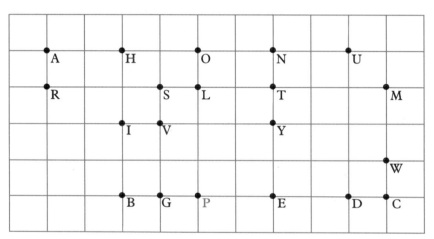

Follow the path given below, beginning at **P**. Follow the numbers in order i.e. do **1**, then do **2** etc. When you have done each one you will come to a letter. Write this letter under the number. For instance, **1** takes you to **I** so write **I** under the number **1** as shown.

1. 2 squares W, then 2 squares N
2. 2 squares N
3. 2 squares E
4. 4 squares S
5. 2 squares E
6. 2 squares N
7. 2 squares W, then 2 squares N
8. 4 squares E
9. 4 squares S
10. 4 squares W, then 4 squares N
11. 2 squares E
12. 1 square S
13. 3 squares S, then 3 squares W
14. 3 squares E
15. 3 squares N
16. 2 squares W
17. 1 square N
18. 1 square W, then 1 square S
19. 3 squares E

GAME 11:7

CROSS – a game for 2 to 5 players.

You will need: a cube
a die
the board on the next page
different coloured counters for each player

First 1. Write S, N, W, E on 4 faces of the cube. Leave the other 2 faces blank.

2. Stick 1, 2 and 3 over the 4, 5 and 6 on the die.

The Game Each player puts a counter on a START square.
These are marked S.
Players take turns to toss the die and the cube.
The cube tells you which direction to move in.
The die tells you how many squares to move.
If you toss a blank face you may choose to move N, S, E *or* W.
Each time you land on a pink square, take 5 points.

Note: If you can't move the number of squares shown on the die you must go to the nearest S square.

The first player to get 20 points is the winner.

continued . . .

... *from previous page*

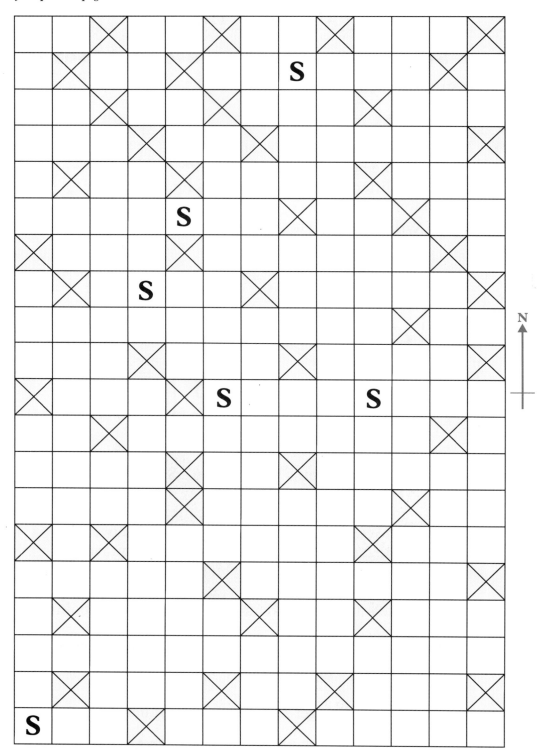

PRACTICAL 11:8

Work In Groups

●   Melanie's group made up a treasure hunt. The first set of instructions was:

Walk out of the classroom.
Walk North until you reach a tall tree.
Turn and walk East until you come to the soccer pitch.
Turn and walk South until you find a tin.
Your next set of directions is in the tin.

Make up your own treasure hunt. Give your directions to another group.

●   Make up a game of your own. Use directions in your game. It might be a card game, a board game or a game that you play outside.
Give your game to another group to play.

READING MAPS

We often show where a place is on a map by using a letter and a number. The letter is usually given first.

Example

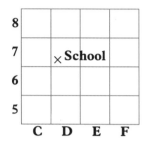

The school is at D7. The school is in the square above D and along from 7. The school could be anywhere in this square and still be at D7.

EXERCISE 11:9

1.

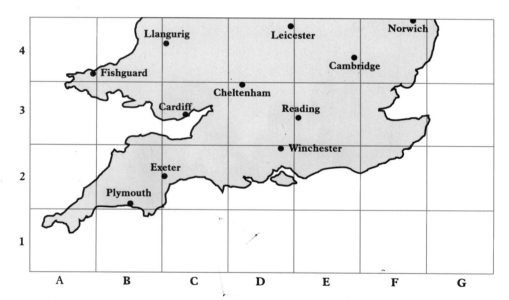

(a) Name the towns which are in these squares. D2, F4, A4.

(b) What square are these in?

| Exeter | Plymouth | Cheltenham |
| Llangurig | Reading | Cambridge |

2.

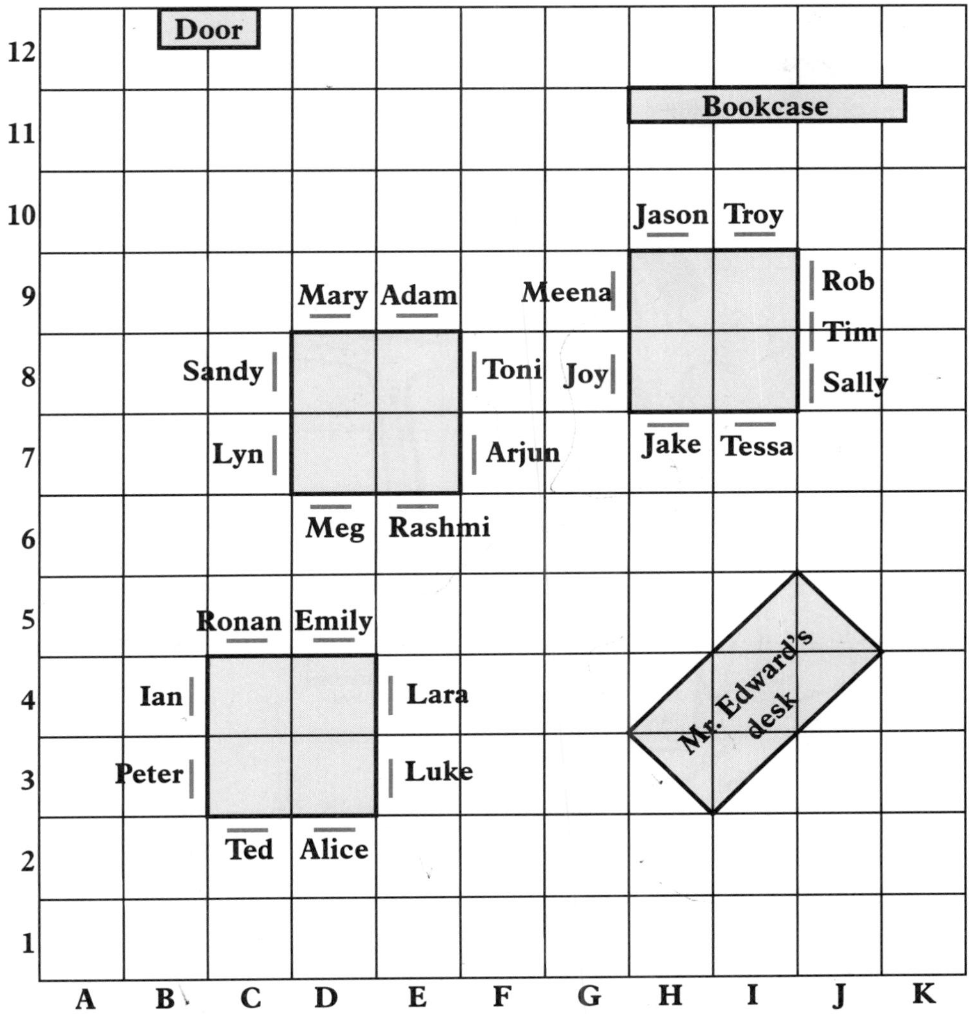

Door — 12

Bookcase — 11

10 — Jason | Troy

9 — Mary | Adam | Meena | Rob

8 — Sandy | Toni | Joy | Tim | Sally

7 — Lyn | Arjun | Jake | Tessa

6 — Meg | Rashmi

5 — Ronan | Emily

4 — Ian | Lara | Mr. Edward's desk

3 — Peter | Luke

2 — Ted | Alice

1

A B C D E F G H I J K

Mr Edward's class divided their classroom up into squares.

(a) Which square do these people sit in?
Emily   Jake   Adam   Arjun   Tim   Joy

(b) Who sits in these squares?
D2, I7, C8, J9, B4, E6

(c) What squares are Mr Edward's desk in?

(d) What squares are the bookcase and door in?

3.

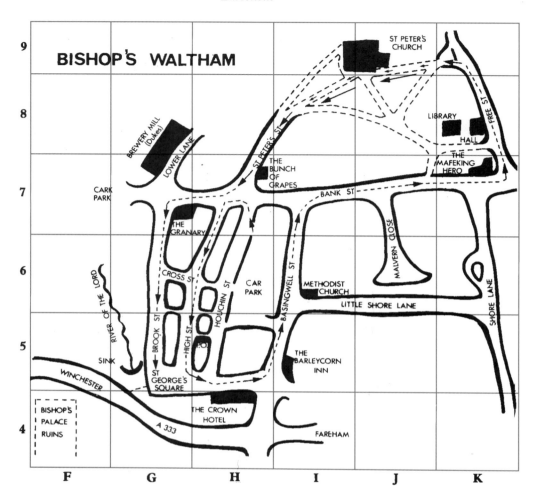

(a) What square are these in?

Library   The Bunch of Grapes

The Granary   Bishop's Palace Ruins

(b) Which church is in square I6?

(c) Which hotel is in square H4?

(d) Which two squares could be used to show where St. Peter's Church is?

(e) What squares are the car parks in?

4.

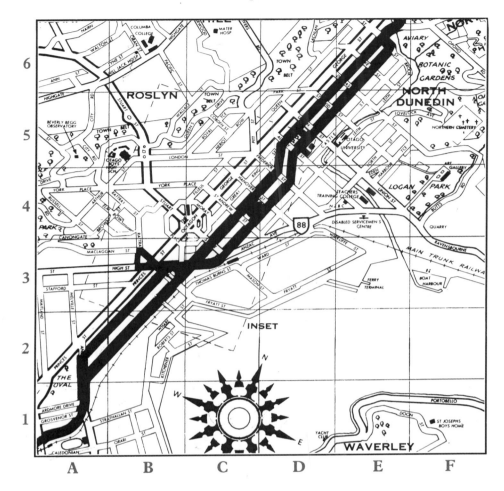

Jane and her penfriend Samantha sent each other a map of where they lived. This is the map that Samantha sent Jane.

(a) What square are these in: Yacht Club
      Ferry Terminal
      Columba College
      Caledonian Ground
      Botanic Gardens

(b) Samantha's brother goes to a school at B5. What school does he go to?

(c) Samantha's sister is a nurse at the hospital in square B6. What hospital is this?

Review

(a) Name the places in squares C4 and B2.

(b) What squares are l'Etacq and Gorey in?

(c) What square is St. Lawrence in?

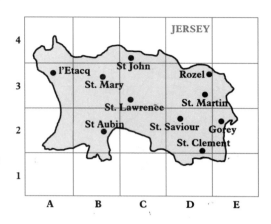

PRACTICAL 11:10

1. Draw a map of your school grounds.

   Make squares on your map. Put letters along the bottom and numbers up the side.

   Write down the squares that parts of your school are in.

2. Write a book about your school.

   In this book, put a map of the school buildings.

   You could also put things such as the following in your book:
   - history of your school
   - clubs for students
   - teachers' names and subjects they teach
   - school hours

continued . . .

. . . from previous page

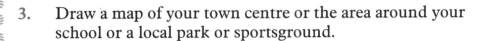

3. Draw a map of your town centre or the area around your school or a local park or sportsground.

    Make squares on your map and use A1, A2 etc on your map.

WORK THIS OUT

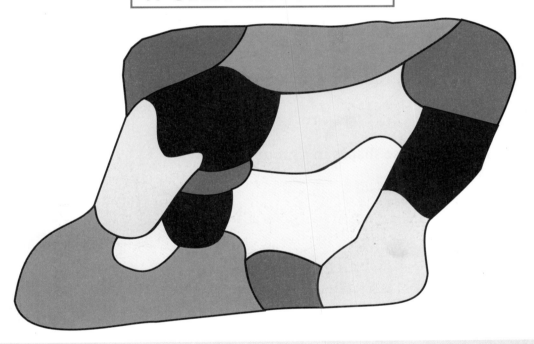

This map has been coloured with 5 colours.
Parts which are next to each other must always be different colours.

This map can be coloured using just 4 colours.
Make a copy of this map and try it.

Can this map be coloured using just 3 colours?

Draw a map that can be coloured using just 3 colours.

Shape, Space and Measures Review

1. Amra put these shapes in a group.

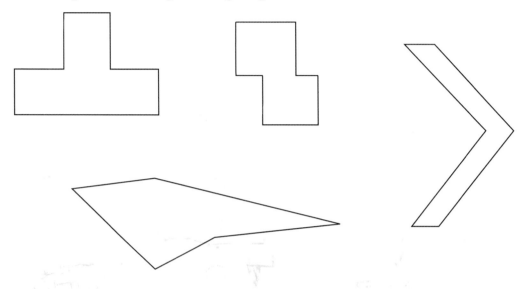

Grace put these shapes in a group.

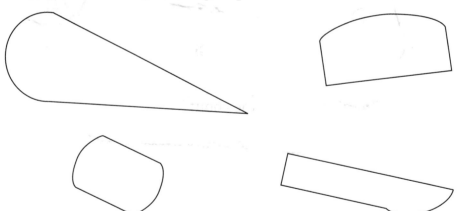

Whose group would this shape belong to? How do you know?

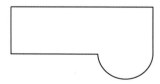

2. Which of the shapes in red have   (a)   no right angles

                                       (b)   4 sides

                                       (c)   one or more curved sides?

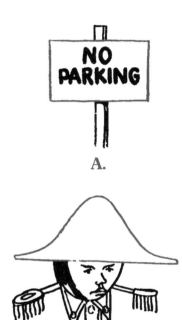

A.

B.

C.

D.

E.

F.

3. The height of a building could be about

   A. 5mm   B. 100cm   C. 30 metres   D. 1 metre.

4. The weight of a large block of cheese could be about

   A. 30g   B. 300kg   C. 1kg   D. 60g.

5. The amount of water in a small fish bowl could be about

   A. 3 litres   B. 100m*l*   C. 100 litres   D. 60m*l*.

6.

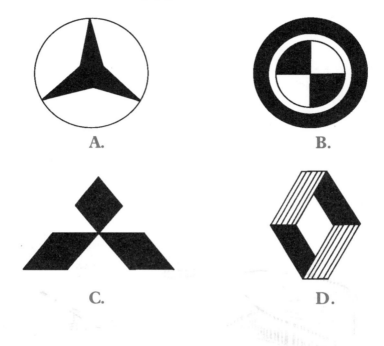

A.   B.

C.   D.

Which of these shapes have   (a)   one line of symmetry

(b)   no line of symmetry

(c)   more than one line of symmetry?

7. Dean faced South. Then he

> walked 10 steps forward
> turned clockwise a half turn
> walked 20 steps forward
> turned anticlockwise through one right angle.

What direction is he facing now?

8.

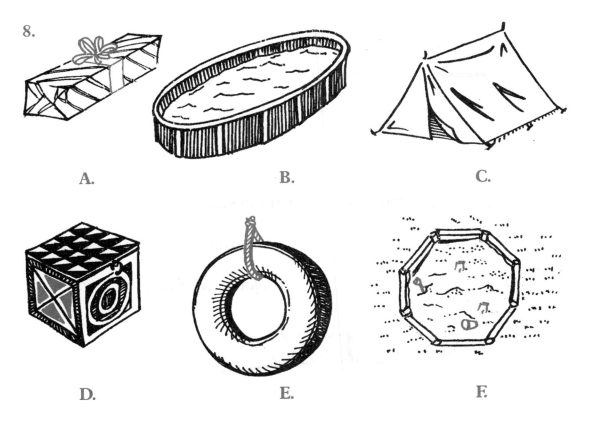

A. B. C.

D. E. F.

Sort these shapes into 4 groups. Some shapes will be in more than one group.

> Group 1: Shapes with fewer than 8 vertices.
> Group 2: Shapes with no vertices.
> Group 3: Shapes with 8 or more vertices.
> Group 4: Shapes with more than 2 planes of symmetry.

What shapes are in (a) Group 1 (b) Group 2 (c) Group 3 (d) Group 4?

9. What do these read to the nearest mark?

(a) 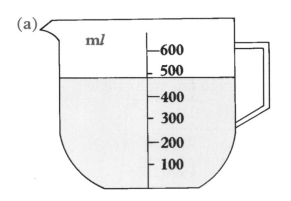 (b)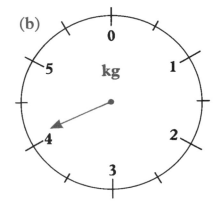

10. This is the timetable for a bus.

TONBRIDGE, Rail Station, Stop H	1743	1758	1813	1829	1843
Tonbridge, Castle, Stop C	1745	1800	1815	1831	1845
Shipbourne Road, The Pinnacles	1750	1805	1820	1836	1850
WILLOWLEA	1758	1813	1826	1842	1856

(a) What time does the bus that leaves Tonbridge at 1843 get to Willowlea?

(b) What time is this in a.m./p.m. time?

11.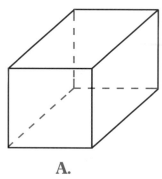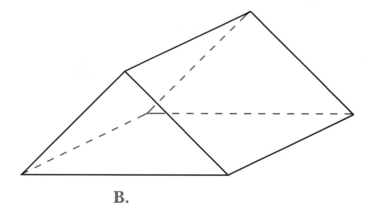

A.   B.

How many faces has   (a)   shape A

                      (b)   shape B?

12.

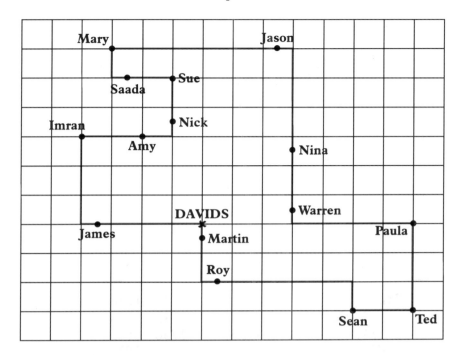

David walked to each of his friend's houses to give them an invitation to his party. The map showing where his friends live is given above. The way David went is shown in red. Finish these directions.

Go West to James' house.
Walk to the corner.
Go North to Imran's house.

13. Which of these has a line or plane of symmetry?

(a)

(b)

(c)

(d)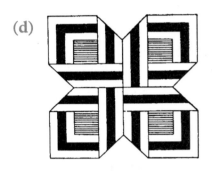

(e)

14. Lance looked at his watch to see if it was time to get up. What time does his watch show?

15. Belinda drew 2 lines on a square to make the 3 shapes shown. What shapes can you make by drawing 2 lines on a square?

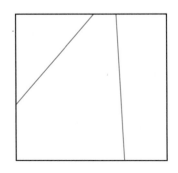

274

16. Garth decided to bake his father a birthday cake. This is the recipe.

GINGER CAKE

125g butter | 300g sugar
2 tbsp golden syrup | 1tsp ginger, mixed spice
200ml of water | and cinnamon
$\frac{1}{2}$ tsp baking soda | 200g self raising flour
2 eggs beaten | $\frac{1}{4}$ tsp salt

(a) Which things would Garth use the kitchen scales for?

(b) Which things would Garth use a measuring jug for?

(c) Garth put the cake in the oven at the temperature shown. What temperature is this?

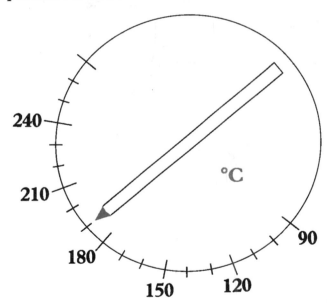

17. Change these to 24-hour clock times.

(a) 1:15 a.m.   (b) 8:20 p.m.   (c) 10:30 a.m.

(d) 12:40 a.m.   (e) 10 to 3 in the afternoon.

18. (a) Which of the following would you use to measure the length of your house?

   A. thumb widths   **B.** strides   **C.** your foot   **D.** your arm

   (b) Explain why measures such as those given in **(a)** are not very accurate.

19. (a) Explain how these patterns have been made using words such as sliding, turning and symmetrical.

   (b) Make a pattern by taking one or two of these shapes and sliding or turning them. You may choose a shape or shapes of your own.

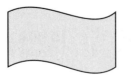   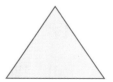

20. Janice measured the width of her thumb. How wide is it?

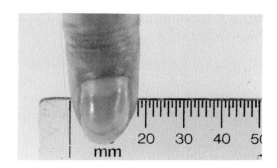

21. Jason walked from his house to the bus stop.

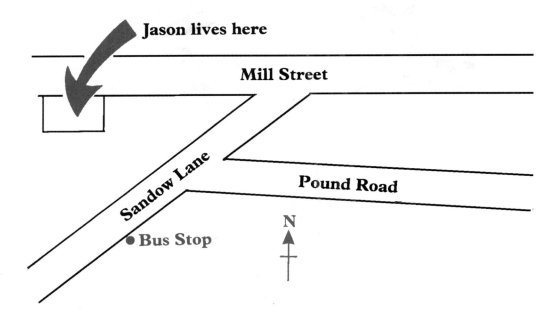

(a) Would Jason turn clockwise or anticlockwise into Sandow Lane?

(b) As Jason walked along Mill Street the sun was shining onto his back. Would the sun shine on the left or right side of Jason's face as he walked along Sandow Lane?

22. Kate has a speedometer on her bicycle.

About what speed is Kate travelling?

23.

kg	m	cm	mm	*l*	m*l*
g	km	hours	seconds	minutes

What would you use to measure these? Choose from the box.

(a) the weight of a paperback book

(b) the time of a telephone call

(c) the amount of water in a tablespoon

(d) the length of the hem on a dress

(e) the weight of a shark

(f) the time to give the answer to 8 + 12 + 4

(g) the amount of petrol in a car

(h) the length of a motorway

(i) the time taken to read a 200 page book

(j) the length of a postcard

(k) the width of a nail

24.

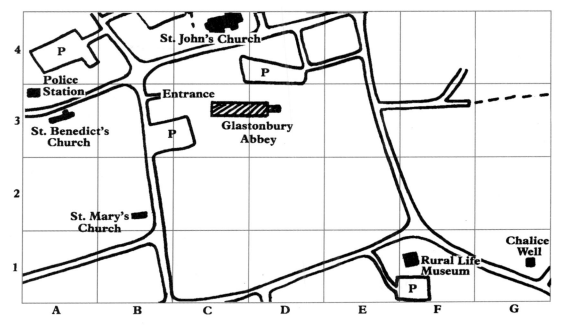

(a) Which church is in square C4?

(b) What squares are these in: Chalice Well
                                     Rural Life Museum
                                     Police Station
                                     St. Mary's Church?

(c) Which two squares could give the location of Glastonbury Abbey?

25. Copy this shape. Add one square to make it symmetrical.

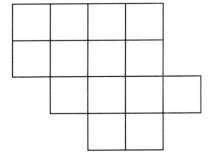

26. How could you take 5 matchsticks from this to leave a symmetrical shape? Is there more than one answer?

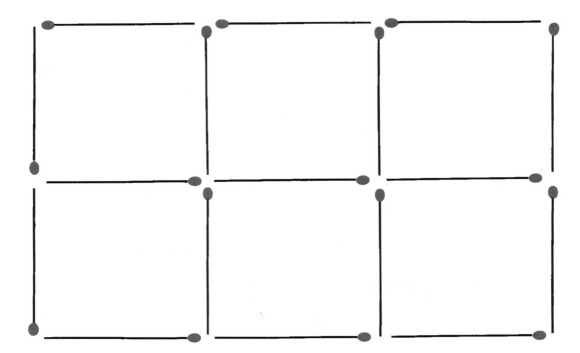

HANDLING DATA

Handling Data from Previous Levels

SORTING

When we **sort** things, we first decide *how* we will sort them.

Example We could sort people into

              male and female
    or the month they were born in
    or tall and short.

COLLECTING

When we collect information it is best to have a **collection sheet**.

We could use a **tally chart**.

Example John asked his friends what sport they liked best.
He drew this tally chart.

Sport	Tally
Football	JHT JHT JHT
Cricket	JHT JHT II
Netball	JHT IIII
Badminton	JHT I
Tennis	JHT JHT I

On the tally chart strokes are put in groups. The 5th stroke is drawn across the first 4. This makes it easy to count up the totals.

continued . . .

. . . *from previous page*

A **frequency table** can be made from a tally chart. We add the tallies to get the frequency.

Sport	Tally	Frequency
Football	ⅲ ⅲ ⅲ	15
Cricket	ⅲ ⅲ ‖	12
Netball	ⅲ ‖‖	9
Badminton	ⅲ ¦	6
Tennis	ⅲ ⅲ ¦	11

SHOWING INFORMATION

Information we collect can be shown on a **block graph**.

Example

Flavour	Chocolate	Caramel	Lime	Strawberry
Number	8	4	3	6

This frequency table shows the milk shake flavour the students in Felicity's class liked best.
This information is shown on the block graph below.

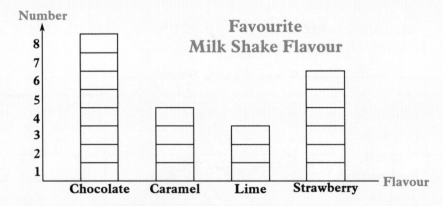

We can make some statements about this graph.

Examples More students like chocolate than caramel.
Lime is the least liked flavour.

continued . . .

. . . *from previous page*

We can show information on a **Venn diagram**.

Students in a class were asked
about T.V. and homework.
This Venn diagram shows that
10 students watched T.V. and did
homework.

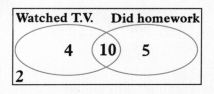

5 students did homework but didn't watch T.V.
4 students watched T.V. but didn't do homework.
2 students neither watched T.V. nor did homework.

This **Carroll Diagram** shows the same information.

	Homework	No homework
Watched T.V.	10	4
Didn't watch T.V.	5	2

This **tree diagram** can be used to sort counters into red and
square, red and round, black and square, black and round.

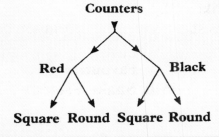

REVISION EXERCISE

1.   Elise wanted to collect information about the number of times
     her teacher said "Quiet please" or "I'm waiting" or "O.K."

     Draw up a tally chart that Elise could use to collect this
     information.

2. Copy the box. Put a line from each object to either rough or smooth.
    The first one is done for you.

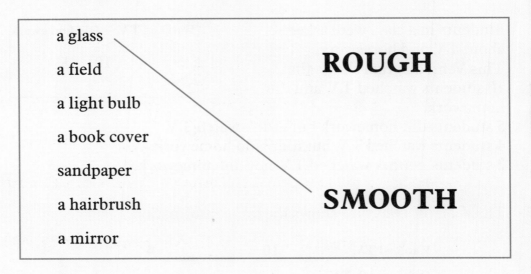

3. Jane has green eyes and brown hair.
    Geoffrey has blue eyes and blond hair.
    Rosalie has blue eyes and brown hair.
    Manoj has brown eyes and black hair.
    Kay has blue eyes and red hair.

    Julia sorted these people by eye colour. What groups would she have?
    Write down another way of sorting these people into groups.

4. This Carroll diagram is for Liz's class.

7	5	Boy
9	2	Girl
Likes maths.	Doesn't like maths.	

    (a) How many boys like maths.?

    (b) How many boys are there in Liz's class?

    (c) How many students like maths.?

    (d) What else can you tell from this diagram?

5.

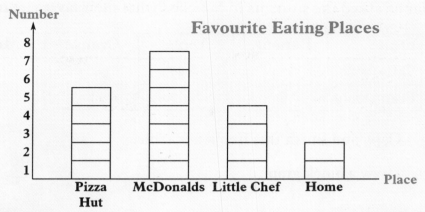

Vicky asked her friends what their favourite eating place was. She drew this block graph.

(a)   Where do the greatest number of Vicky's friends like to eat?

(b)   Where do the least number like to eat?

(c)   Which place do 4 of Vicky's friends like best?

(d)   What else can you tell from this graph?

6.   Some students in Vanessa's class have

a brother and a sister
a brother but no sister
a sister but no brother
neither a brother nor a sister.

Copy and finish this tree diagram to sort the students into groups.

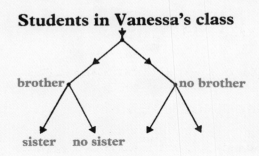

7. Dianne asked the students in her class what their favourite fruit was.

Fruit	**Banana**	**Apple**	**Orange**	**Melon**
Tally	⩘ ∥	⩘ ⩘	⩘ ∥	∥
Frequency	7			

(a) Copy and finish this frequency table.

(b) Draw a block graph.

8.

raining   windy

11 8 5

7

Martin collected information about the weather in January. He drew this Venn diagram.

On how many days was it

(a) both raining and windy   (b) raining but not windy

(c) neither raining nor windy   (d) windy but not raining?

9. In Verity's class   12 played a winter and a summer sport
6 played a winter but not a summer sport
5 played a summer but not a winter sport
2 played neither a summer nor a winter sport.

Show this information on a Carroll diagram.

Weekends

DISCUSSION AND PRACTICAL 13:1

● "I used a bus timetable to go skating," said Evan.
"I looked up the prices of fishing rods," said Ajit.
"I worked out when I could go to the swimming pool and
how much it would cost," said Emily.

What do you do in the weekend? Think of when you use a
table, a chart or a list to find information. **Discuss.**

● Plan a weekend doing the things you enjoy most. Find out
the information you need. Think about

　　　　　　times
　　　　　　how to get there
　　　　　　costs

Make a poster or collage or give a talk about your weekend.
Show all the timetables, charts and lists you used.

READING TABLES, CHARTS and LISTS

DISCUSSION 13:2

GYMKHANA
EVENTS 5-15

**ENTRIES MAY ONLY BE MADE ON THE
DAY OF THE SHOW AT THE COLLECTING RING**
Judging to commence after Event 4 (Chase Me Charlie)
at approx 3.30 p.m. Ring 3
Entry fee: 50p. in all events
Prizes: 1st - £3. 2nd - £2. 3rd - £1. 4th - 50p.

EVENT	5	**WALK AND TROT COMPETITION, Age 3 - 9**
EVENT	6	**DISPATCH RACE, Age 3 - 9**
EVENT	7	**GREEDY PONY, Age 3 - 9·**
EVENT	8	**BENDING COMPETITION, Age 10 - 13**
EVENT	9	**POTATO RACE, Age 10 - 13**
EVENT	10	**WALK, TROT AND CANTER, Age 10 - 13**
EVENT	11	**BENDING COMPETITION, Age 14 and over**
EVENT	12	**POTATO RACE, Age 14 and over**
EVENT	13	**WALK, TROT AND CANTER, Age 14 and over**
EVENT	14	**GRETNA GREEN, Age under 14**
EVENT	15	**GRETNA GREEN, Age over 14**

"What is event 9?" asked Kate.

"How much do I have to pay to enter 4 events?" asked Jeremy.

What other questions could you answer from this information? Discuss.

continued . . .

. . . *from previous page*

Sheffield Park	dep	10.15	11.00	11.45	12.30	1.15	2.00	2.45	3.30	4.15	5.30	Sheffield Park
Horsted Keynes	arr	10.30	11.15	12.00	12.45	1.30	2.15	3.00	3.45	4.30	5.45	Horsted Keynes
Horsted Keynes	dep	10.35	11.20	12.05	12.50	1.35	2.20	3.05	3.50	4.35	—	Horsted Keynes
New Coombe Bridge	arr	10.45	11.30	12.15	1.00	1.45	2.30	3.15	4.00	4.45	—	New Coombe Bridge
New Coombe Bridge	dep	—	10.55	11.40	12.25	1.10	1.55	2.40	3.25	4.10	4.55	New Coombe Bridge
Horsted Keynes	arr	—	11.03	11.48	12.33	1.18	2.03	2.48	3.33	4.18	5.03	Horsted Keynes
Horsted Keynes	dep	10.32	11.17	12.02	12.47	1.32	2.17	3.02	3.47	4.32	5.07	Horsted Keynes
Sheffield Park	arr	10.45	11.30	12.15	1.00	1.45	2.30	3.15	4.00	4.45	5.20	Sheffield Park

This is the timetable for a train. Plan a day trip from Sheffield Park to New Coombe Bridge and back again. Stop at Horsted Keynes to have lunch. **Discuss.**

PRACTICAL 13:3

Choose a subject such as

sport	world records	food
concerts	holidays	buses
trains	planes	Christmas

Find or make up as many tables, charts and lists as you can about this subject.

Make a leaflet or poster about the subject you have chosen. Use the tables, charts and lists you found or made.

Plan a class journey to somewhere special. Use timetables and price lists to find the information you need.

Make a notice to go home telling your family about the journey, the cost and the timetable.

EXERCISE 13:4

1.

Lamb Cutlet, Bacon, Egg, Sausage, Pudding, Peas & Chips	£6·10
Half Chicken, Slice of Bacon, Chips & Peas	£5·30
Chicken Nuggets, Peas & Chips	£4·10
Chicken Kiev, Salad, Mash or Chips	£4·40
Chicken Burger & Chips	£2·90
Chicken Curry, Rice or Chips	£4·40

Zoe had the Lamb Cutlet and Zuleka had the Chicken Burger. How much did this cost altogether?

2. (a) What time does the first race start on July 31?

(b) What day of the week is the race meeting on 25 September?

(c) On what dates does the first race start at 2·15 p.m.?

(d) What date was Easter Monday in 1993?

Race Fixtures 1993

DAY	DATE	FIRST RACE STARTS AT
THU	7 JAN	1.00 pm
SAT	16 JAN	1.10 pm
SAT	27 FEB	2.25 pm
FRI	12 MARCH	2.00 pm
East MON	12 APRIL	2.15 pm
SAT	24 APRIL	2.15 pm
SAT	8 MAY (Ev)	5.45 pm
SAT	31 JUL (Ev)	6.15 pm
SAT	14 AUG (Ev)	5.35 pm
SAT	18 SEPT	2.15 pm
SAT	25 SEPT	2.20 pm
FRI	8 OCT	2.10 pm
FRI	5 NOV	1.10 pm
SAT	20 NOV	12.40 pm
FRI	17 DEC	12.40 pm
BOXING DAY (Mon)	27 DEC	12.55 pm

FREE CAR PARKING

3.

Black and White	**Colour**
Small: *13cm x 18cm (5" x 7")* **£3.50 £2.80***	***Small:*** *13cm x 18cm (5" x 7")* **£4.50 £3.50***
Medium: *17cm x 22cm (6" x 8")* **£4.00 £3.20***	***Medium:*** *17cm x 22cm (6" x 8")* **£6.50 £5.50***
Large: *20cm x 25cm (8" x 10")* **£6.00 £4.80***	***Large:*** *20cm x 25cm (8" x 10")* **£9.00 £7.00***
* 3 or more prints from the one negative.	** 3 or more prints from the one negative.*

These give the prices of black and white and colour photos for different sizes.

(a) How much does one small black and white photo cost?

(b) What size are the medium black and white photos?

(c) How much would 3 large colour prints of the same photo cost?

(d) Andrea had one medium colour photo made. Bryan had one medium black and white photo made. How much more did it cost Andrea?

(e) Shadia wanted 2 large colour prints of her dog. How much would this cost?

4. **Lighting up** London 8.43pm to 5.10am, Manchester 9.00pm to 5.10am. **Sun rises** 5.12am, **sets** 8.43pm. **Moon rises** 1.48am, **sets** 12.19pm. **High water** London Bridge 7.41am (6.3m), 7.48pm (6.0m); Bristol 12.36am (10.5m), 1.00pm (10.0m); Liverpool 4.55am (7.9m), 5.34pm (7.3m).

IN BRITAIN YESTERDAY

Warmest ....Southend-on-Sea 68F (20C)
Coldest (day) ....Lerwick 46F (8C)
Wettest...Plymouth 0.72 in
Sunniest ....Tiree 14.7 hrs

BRITISH READINGS

Last night's report for 24 hours to 6pm:

	Sun hrs	Rain in	Max °F	°C	Weather (day)
London	4.5	.01	68	20	bright pm
					(Min temp 50F 10C)
Manchester	10.0	—	63	17	sunny
					(Min temp 50F 10C)
Birmingham	7.9	.01	66	19	sunny am
Buxton	9.4	—	57	14	sunny
Leeds	3.7	—	54	12	cloudy
Nottingham	11.9	—	64	18	sunny
East					
Tynemouth	—	—	46	8	dull
Scarboro	4.4	—	50	10	cloudy
Skegness	11.9	.01	55	13	sunny
Hunstanton	9.8	.01	55	13	sunny
Cromer	10.9	—	57	14	sunny
Lowestoft	10.6	—	55	13	sunny
Clacton	9.3	—	64	18	sunny
Southend	3.0	—	68	20	sunny
Herne Bay	1.8	—	57	14	cloudy
Margate	2.6	—	55	13	cloudy
South					
Folkestone	1.6	—	61	16	cloudy

	Sun	Rain	°F	°C	
Hastings	1.0	.03	66	19	rain am
Eastbourne	—	.09	61	16	rain am
Worthing	0.3	—	63	17	cloudy
Littleh'ton	—	.01	63	17	showers am
Bognor	0.4	.02	61	16	showers am
Southsea	0.1	.23	61	16	rain am
Ryde	0.2	.10	61	16	showers
Sandown	0.6	.04	61	16	rain am
Shanklin	0.4	.02	61	16	rain am
Ventnor	0.7	—	61	16	cloudy
Bournem'th	—	.02	61	16	showers
Poole	—	—	61	16	cloudy
Swanage	—	—	59	15	dull
Weymouth	—	.19	57	14	rain
Exmouth	0.1	.21	55	13	rain
Teignmouth	0.1	.57	55	13	rain
Torquay	0.9	.50	55	13	rain pm
Plymouth	1.2	.72	54	12	rain
Falmouth	1.3	—	59	15	cloudy
Penzance	6.6	—	63	17	bright
Isles of Scilly	3.7	—	61	16	bright
Guernsey	9.0	—	66	19	sunny
Jersey	11.9	—	66	19	sunny
West					
Newquay	—	.19	—	—	drizzle pm
Sauntn Snds	2.6	—	61	16	dull
Minehead	0.9	.07	59	15	showers pm
Southport	10.0	—	66	19	sunny

	Sun	Rain	°F	°C	
Morecambe	10.3	—	64	18	sunny
Isle of Man	4.0	.02	63	17	showers pm
Lake District					
Kendal	7.4	—	64	18	sunny
Keswick	7.3	—	66	19	sunny
Ambleside	7.2	—	64	18	sunny
Aspatria	11.7	—	59	15	sunny
Wales					
Anglesey	8.2	—	66	19	sunny pm
Cardiff	0.3	.06	59	15	thunder
Colwyn Bay	6.1	—	61	16	sunny
Tenby	—	.01	57	14	cloudy
Scotland					
Aberdeen	—	—	48	9	dull
Aviemore	4.2	—	50	10	bright pm
Edinburgh	0.8	—	50	10	dull
Eskdalemuir	1.0	—	48	9	cloudy
Lerwick	—	.02	46	8	drizzle
Leuchars	11.8	—	52	11	sunny
Kinloss	0.5	—	50	10	drizzle am
Stornoway	3.5	—	48	9	cloudy
Tiree	14.7	—	55	13	sunny
Wick	—	—	46	8	dull
Northern Ireland					
Belfast	12.6	—	63	17	sunny

(a) Which place was the sunniest? How many hours of sunshine did it have?

(b) Which places had drizzle on this day?

(c) What time did the moon rise and set?

(d) Which place had a temperature of 12°C and rain?

(e) How much hotter was it in Penzance than in Weymouth?

(f) Which places had no sunshine?

(g) What was the weather like in Aberdeen?

(h) Was this weather report for January or May? How do you know?

5.

| Evening Buses |

Gravesend ⟷ Borough Green

Bus
308

Please Note ... These Evening buses are provided on behalf of Kent County Council by Transcity Link (Telephone: 081-302-8800), NOT M&D.

Monday to Saturday Buses:				
GRAVESEND, St. Georges Centre	1907	2007	2107	2207
Gravesend, King Street	1908	2008	2108	2208
Gravesend, Rail Station	1909	2009	2109	2209
Tollgate, Chalky Bank	1914	2014	2114	2214
Istead Rise. Upper Avenue	1917	2017	2117	2217
Istead Rise. Downs Road School	1919	2019	2119	2219
Meopham, Rail Station	1922	2022	2122	2222
Meopham Parade	1924	2024	2124	2224
Meopham, Green	1926	2026	2126	2226
Culverstone School	1928	2028	2128	2228
Vigo, Trosley Country Park	1930	2030	2130	2230
VIGO, Erskine Road, The Bay	1932	2032	2132	2232

Monday to Saturday Buses:				
BOROUGH GREEN, Station	1804	—	—	—
Wrotham Square	1811	—	—	—
Vigo Inn	1816	—	—	—
Vigo, Trosley Country Park	1817	1930	2030	2130
Vigo, Erskine Road, The Bay	1819	1932	2032	2132
Culverstone School	1822	1935	2035	2135
Meopham Green	1825	1938	2038	2138
Meopham Parade	1828	1941	2041	2141
Meopham, Rail Station	1830	1943	2043	2143
Istead Rise, Downs Road School	1833	1946	2046	2146
Istead Rise, Upper Avenue	1835	1948	2048	2148
Tollgate, Chalky Bank	1838	1951	2051	2151
Gravesend, Rail Station	1844	1957	2057	2157
GRAVESEND, St. Georges Centre	1846	1959	2059	2159

(a) Beatrice caught the bus that leaves Gravesend, St. Georges Centre at 2007. What time did she arrive at Culverstone School?

(b) Ameen caught the bus that left Gravesend, Rail Station at 1909 to Meopham, Green. He caught the next bus back to Gravesend. What time did it leave Meopham, Green?

(c) How many buses leave Borough Green Station after 1800?

(d) A bus arrives at Tollgate at 1951. What time did this bus leave Culverstone School?

6.

1993 DAY VISIT PRICES			
Duration	Opening Times	Age 4 Upwards	Age 2/3 Years
Sats & Suns 23 Jan - 7 Feb	10am - 9.30pm Last entry 4pm	£3.50	£3.00
Half Term 13 - 28 Feb	10am - 9.30pm Last entry 4pm	£3.99	£3.00
Daily 13 - 21 Mar	10am - 9.30pm Last entry 4pm	£3.99	£3.00
Sat & Sun 27 - 28 Mar	10am - 9.30pm Last entry 4pm	£3.99	£3.00
Easter - Daily 3 - 16 Apr	10am - 9.30pm Last entry 4pm	£6.50	£3.00
Daily 17 - 23 Apr	10am - 6.00pm Last entry 4pm	£4.99	£3.00
Daily 24 Apr - 16 Jul	10am - 9.30pm Last entry 5pm	£5.99	£3.00
Daily 17 Jul - 3 Sept	10am - 9.30pm Last entry 5pm	£6.50	£3.00
Daily 4 Sept - 29 Oct	10am - 9.30pm Last entry 5pm	£5.99	£3.00
Bank Holiday Sundays/Mondays & Good Friday	**As Applicable**	**£6.99**	**£3.00**

This table gives the 1993 prices and opening times for Butlins.

(a) How much would it cost for two adults on April 16?

(b) What are the opening times for Butlins on Aug 12?

(c) What is the latest time you could go into Butlins on Feb 2?

(d) Debbie's cousins spent the day at Butlins on Sept 3. How much would it cost for this family of two adults and two children aged 3 and 5?

(e) How much less would it cost if the same family went on Sept 4?

7. The Sansom family bought some Christmas presents from a mail-order booklet. They wrote down this list. Copy and fill in the costs.

For	Present	Cost
Susannah	Bubble Jumper	
Paula and Lucy	Playtent	
Andrew	Spiralmatic	
	Total	

Review 1

| FROM DUBLIN TO LONDON | FROM LONDON TO DUBLIN |

DUBLIN TO LONDON STANSTED

Flight Number	Depart	Arrive	Frequency
FR202	0725	0835	M T W T F S -
FR204	0855	1005	M T W T F S -
FR206	1055	1205	M T W T F S S
FR208	1155	1305	M T W T F S S
FR212	1255	1405	M T W T F - -
FR214	1355	1505	- - - - - - S
FR216	1455	1605	M T W T F S S
FR218	1655	1805	M T W T F S S
FR222	1755	1905	M T W T F - S
FR224	1855	2005	M T W T F - S
FR226	1955	2105	M T W T F - S

LONDON STANSTED TO DUBLIN

Flight Number	Depart	Arrive	Frequency
FR203	0745	0855	M T W T F - -
FR205	0915	1025	M T W T F S -
FR207	1045	1155	M T W T F S -
FR209	1245	1355	M T W T F S S
FR211	1445	1555	M T W T F - -
FR213	1545	1655	- - - - - - S
FR215	1645	1755	M T W T F S S
FR217	1745	1855	M T W T F S S
FR219	1845	1955	M T W T F S S
FR221	1945	2055	M T W T F - S
FR223	2045	2155	M T W T F - S
FR225	2145	2255	- - - - F - -

This is the Ryanair plane timetable between London and Dublin.

(a) Russell wanted to get to Dublin as early as possible one Tuesday morning. What time would his plane leave London Stansted?

(b) On what days of the week does a plane leave Dublin at 1255 for London?

(c) What time does the flight that leaves London Stansted at 2145 get to Dublin?

(d) On which day (or days) does flight FR213 fly?

(e) Siobhan wanted to spend at least 4 hours in London one Sunday. She arrived on flight FR206. Which is the earliest flight she could catch back to Dublin?

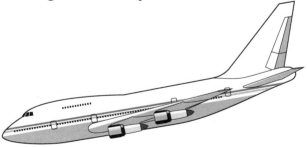

Review 2

BARGAIN FARES

FOOT PASSENGERS	Adult	Child (4-16)	Family
DAY RETURN	£11	£6	£30
EARLY RISER day return	£9	£6	£25
DAY RETURN including entrance to Nausicaa	£16	£9	£45
OVERNIGHTERS	£16	£9	£39
CAR AND UP TO 5 PASSENGERS	Depart Fridays and Saturdays		Depart Other Days
DAY RETURN off peak	£79		£69
DAY RETURN peak	N/A		£79
OVERNIGHT RETURN off peak	£119		£99
OVERNIGHT RETURN peak	N/A		£119

Peak = 01/07 to 05/09

Children under 4 not occupying a seat go FREE

This chart shows the hovercraft bargain fares from Dover to Calais.

(a) How much does an adult day return cost?

(b) How much does an early riser family ticket cost?

(c) How much would it cost to take a car overnight return on a Thursday in March?

(d) What would a family without a car have to pay for an overnighter?

(e) Would it be cheaper for a family of 2 adults and 2 children aged 3 and 5 to buy a family ticket or pay the adult and child prices for an early riser?

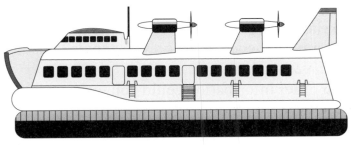

MORE TABLES

Sometimes we collect 2 bits of information about something.
These can be put onto a table.

Example   Dale asked the students at his school what music they liked best
and what year they were in. He put his results on this table.

	Piano	Guitar	Saxophone	Drums	Violin	Other	None	Totals
Year 7	21	49	32	24	15	62	12	
Year 8	9	54	23	40	21	19	39	
Year 9	41	63	11	22	13	49	23	
Totals								

DISCUSSION 13:5

Look at the table above for this exercise.

● "54 people in Year 8 liked guitar music best", said Anya.
"166 people that Dale asked liked guitar music best", said Eric.
"Dale asked 205 Year 8 students about music", said Syeda.

How did Anya, Eric and Syeda work this out from the table?
Discuss.

Make 3 more statements like Anya's, Eric and Syeda's.
Discuss.

Make a copy of this table. Add up the totals.
What number goes in the grey rectangle? Discuss.

● What other information could you put on a table like the one above? Discuss.

EXERCISE 13:6

1.

Shop \ Item	Jeans	Skirts	Shorts	Tops	Totals
TOP SHOP SALES			22nd April		
Westvale	14	8	4	15	
Sunhill	9	6	3	9	
Beachville	11	12	7	17	
Dumfrey	23	20	11	14	
Totals					

This table shows the number of jeans, skirts, shorts and tops sold by four TOP SHOPS on the 22nd of April.

(a)   How many skirts did the Beachville shop sell?

(b)   Which shop sold the smallest number of jeans?

(c)   How many tops were sold altogether by the 4 shops?

(d)   Copy the table. Add up the totals. What number goes in the grey box?

2.

Throw \ Die	White	Red	Black	Totals
1st	3	4	6	
2nd	1	1	5	
Totals				

A white, red and black die are tossed twice. This table shows the numbers tossed.

(a)   Copy the table. Add up the totals. What number goes in the grey box?

(b)   Which die had the highest total for 2 throws?

3. Victoria asked some students at her school when they used the library. Her results are shown.

	Monday	Tuesday	Wednesday	Thursday	Friday	Totals
Before school	34	29	23	54	52	
Lunch time	81	72	59	62	44	
After school	18	27	6	23	12	
Totals	133	128	88	139	108	

(a) Copy this table. Add up the totals. What number goes in the grey box?

(b) What can Victoria say about the times students use the library?

Review

Extras ＼ Pizza	Meat Feast	Supreme	Vegetarian	Pan Pizza	Totals
Salad	2	4	0	5	
Garlic Bread	1	3	2	6	
Totals					

This table shows what the students in Sandra's class ordered from Pizza Hut. Each student had Pizza and either salad or bread.

(a) Copy the table. Add up the totals. What number goes in the grey box?

(b) How many Pan Pizzas did these students order?

(c) How many students had garlic bread?

(d) How many students from Sandra's class went to Pizza Hut?

PRACTICAL 13:7

Think of information you could collect to put on a table like the ones in **Exercise 13:6**.
Think of a way to collect this information.
Collect the data and show it on a table.

DATABASES

When files or computers store information about people, animals, jobs or something else, this is called a **database**.

Example   Many cards with information like this, kept in a file, make up a card database.

NAME:	WINNIE PEG
ADDRESS:	67 LIVERPOOL PLACE CHATHILL
AGE:	67
HAIR:	GREY

DISCUSSION 13:8

● "My doctor keeps the information about her patients in a database," said Kate.

"I think a hospital would have to keep its information on a database," said Matthew.

Melanie, Sandy, Tim, Annabel and Anjuli gave examples of other databases. What might these have been? Discuss.

● What information about your class could be stored in a database? Discuss.

Make up some information that might be in a database for your school. Discuss.

EXERCISE 13:9

1. This table shows the information in a database.

   (a) How many children have a cat?

   (b) How many children have rabbits?

Name	Age	Pet
Tracey White	10	Rabbit
John West	11	Cat
Faye Moore	11	Dog
Hood Tull	12	Rabbit

   (c) What are the names of the children with rabbits?

   (d) What are the names of the 11-year-olds on this database?

2.

Where last holiday was spent			
Name	Age	Holiday Place	Month
Mrs Green	53	Spain	Sept
Mandy	22	Ireland	April
Thomas	16	France	Oct
Ismail	35	Devon	Sept
Mr Taylor	64	Lake District	Sept

   Erika asked some of the people in her street where they went for their last holiday. She put the information into this database.

   (a) How many people had a holiday in September?

   (b) Where did Thomas spend his holiday?

   (c) Write down the list of people who had a holiday in September.

   (d) Write down the list of people who had a holiday abroad.

   (e) Write down the list of people under 20 years of age.

3. This table is a copy of a database.

Members of The Garden Club			
Name	M/F	Town/City	Garden type
Edna Porter	F	Rayleigh	Herb
Paran Jeet	M	Southend-on-Sea	Herb
Holly Turner	F	Hockley	Rose
Luke Walker	M	Brentwood	Dahlia
Dale Lang	F	Rayleigh	Rose
Joyce Sansom	F	Rayleigh	Herb

(a) What does M/F mean?

(b) Write down the list of people who have rose gardens.

(c) Write down the list of people who live in Rayleigh.

(d) Write down the list of women.

(e) Write down the list of men who have herb gardens.

Review This table shows the information stored in a database.

Month of Birth		
Name	Age	Birth Month
Joshua Topp	10	September
Rebecca Turpin	11	May
Nema Ghan	10	May
Heidi Deitrich	12	April
Adam Brown	10	September

(a) How many 10-year-olds are there on this database?

(b) Write down the list of people who were born in September.

(c) Write down the list of 10-year-olds.

(d) Write down the list of 10-year-olds born in May.

PRACTICAL 13:10

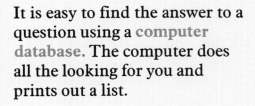

Work In Groups

What information would you like to know about your class?
Collect this information. You might collect information about

       hair colour
       eye colour
       birthdate
       height
       favourite colour
       favourite drink
       favourite icecream
       pets
       sport played

Make a card database from the information you collected.

Think of some questions you could answer using your database.
These might be   How many have a pet?
                Which students are taller than 145cm?
                How many like red best?

Use your database to find the answers to your questions.

It is easy to find the answer to a question using a computer database. The computer does all the looking for you and prints out a list.

PRACTICAL 13:11

Use a database on your computer for this exercise.

- Your school will most likely have databases with information already stored.

  Find out how to use one of these on your computer.

  You can use the computer to search through the database to answer questions.

  For example, if your database has information about capitals and populations of countries, you could ask the computer to print the names of countries with a population over 5,000,000.

```
        POPULATIONS  OF  NORTH  EUROPEAN  COUNTRIES


      COUNTRY                 CAPITAL          POPULATION
  - - - - - - - - - - -     - - - - - - -     - - - - - - - -
  BELGIUM                   BRUSSELS          9,881,000
  DENMARK                   COPENHAGEN        5,141,000
  ENGLAND                   LONDON            47,536,000
  FINLAND                   HELSINKI          4,971,000
  NETHERLANDS               AMSTERDAM         14,927,000
  NORTHERN  IRELAND         BELFAST           1,578,000
  REPUBLIC  OF  IRELAND     DUBLIN            3,509,000
  SCOTLAND                  EDINBURGH         5,094,000
  WALES                     CARDIFF           2,857,000
```

Find out how to search *your* database for information you want.
Try finding the answers to lots of questions.
How do you print these out?

continued . . .

. . . from previous page

● Set up your own database on the computer. Decide what information you will put into the database. You could use the same information you put onto the card database in **Practical 13:10.** You could collect information about

school lunches   another class   animals

Put the information into the database.

What questions could you answer using your database?
Write these down.
You might want to answer
　　— how many have blue eyes?
　　— how many have blue eyes and blond hair?
　　— do students with brown hair play more sport?

Print out your information.
Make a poster, mural, booklet or give a talk about the information you found out.

WORK THIS OUT

These are the charts from three car rental firms.

DRIVEAWAY		
per day	3 days	7 days
£28	£71	£135
+ petrol Drive as many km as you like		

EASY DRIVE
per day £12
plus 10p each kilometre + petrol

SAVE AND DRIVE		
per day	3 days	7 days
£15	£33	£95
+6p per kilometre +petrol		

Susan wanted to hire a car for 7 days. She decided it was cheapest from "Save and Drive".

What is the greatest number of kilometres she planned to drive?

Look Around You at . . .

Early Life on Earth

PRACTICAL AND DISCUSSION 14:1

- Before the alphabet was made up, people wrote down information using pictures.
  Find out as much as you can about early picture writing.
  Discuss what you found with your group.

- Write down some information about yourself and your family using pictures. See if your group can "read" your pictures.

- "I think early people used a type of graph to keep track of numbers of things like animals," said Alana.

  What is a **graph**? What sorts of graphs do you think early people might have used? **Discuss.**

- Make a poster, mural or collage about picture information.

PICTOGRAMS

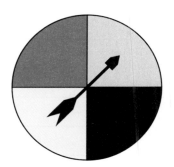

A spinner was spun 50 times. This table shows the results.

Colour	Number of Times
Red	10
Grey	14
Pink	11
Black	15

Here is another way of showing the same information.

Colour	Number of Times
Red	⊕⊕⊕⊕⊕
Grey	⊕⊕⊕⊕⊕⊕⊕
Pink	⊕⊕⊕⊕⊕∈
Black	⊕⊕⊕⊕⊕⊕⊕∈
	Key: ⊕ = 2 times

Which way do you think is more interesting?
What do you think ∈ stands for?
Why do we need a key? **Discuss.**

continued . . .

. . . *from previous page*

BAYFIELD HIGH SCHOOL

Match Date	Runs in Cricket
Feb 14	ᵻᵻᵻᵻᵻᵻᵻᵻᵻ
Feb 21	ᵻᵻᵻᵻᵻᵻᵻ
Mar 7	ᵻᵻᵻᵻᵻᵻᵻᵻᵻᵻᵻ
Mar 14	ᵻᵻᵻᵻᵻ
Mar 21	ᵻᵻᵻᵻᵻᵻᵻᵻᵻ
	Key: ᵻ **= 10 runs**

What do you think ⌐ means? **Discuss.**

What information does this graph tell you? **Discuss.**

A **pictogram** is a picture graph. It always has a key which tells you what each small picture stands for.

Example   This pictogram shows the number of animals in a pet holiday home. There are 24 cats, 14 dogs, 6 rabbits and 2 birds.

Animal	Number
Cat	🐈🐈🐈🐈🐈🐈
Dog	🐈🐈🐈🐈
Rabbit	🐈🐈
Bird	🐈
	Key: 🐈 **= 4 animals**

EXERCISE 14:3

Day	Number of Students
Monday	🚶🚶🚶🚶🚶
Tuesday	🚶🚶🚶
Wednesday	🚶🚶🚶🚶
Thursday	🚶🚶🚶🚶🚶
Friday	🚶🚶🚶🚶🚶🚶🚶
	Key: 🚶 = 2 students

1. This pictogram shows the number of students away from school one week in March.

    (a) How many students were away on Wednesday?

    (b) Which day had the most students away?

    (c) How many more students were away on Friday than on Monday?

    (d) There were 2 students away in Morgan's class on Thursday. How many students were away from other classes on this day?

    (e) What else does this pictogram tell you?

2.

Favourite Drink	No. of Students
Milk Shake	🥛🥛🥛🥛🥛🥛
Coke	🥛🥛🥛🥛🥛🥛🥛
Water	🥛🥛🥛
Milk	🥛🥛
Lemonade	🥛🥛🥛🥛🥛
Other fizzy drink	🥛🥛🥛🥛🥛🥛🥛🥛
	Key: 🥛 = 4 students

This pictogram shows the favourite drink of some students.

    (a) How many students were asked about their favourite drink?

    (b) How many students like coke best?

(c) How many students like water best?

(d) How many students like some sort of fizzy drink best? (Coke or Lemonade or other fizzy drink)

(e) 24 students like lemonade best. How many more students like coke best?

(f) What else does this pictogram tell you?

3. Megan was doing a survey on cars. She drew this pictogram to show the colour of cars that passed the school gate in one hour.

Colour	Number of Cars
Red	
White	
Green	
Blue	
Brown	
Grey	
Yellow	

Key: = 10 cars

(a) How many cars of each colour were there?

(b) How many more red than yellow cars passed the school?

(c) How many cars passed the school gate altogether?

(d) What else does this pictogram tell you?

4.

Day	Number of Packets
Monday	55
Tuesday	40
Wednesday	60
Thursday	50
Friday	55

This table shows the number of packets of crisps sold at the school shop one week. Copy and finish the pictogram.

Day	Number of Packets
Monday	▢ ▢ ▢ ▢ ▢ ▢
Tuesday	▢ ▢ ▢ ▢
Wednesday	
Thursday	
Friday	
	Key: ▢ = 10 Packets

5. Sam asked each of his friends what type of book they liked best. This table shows his results.

Book	Science Fiction	Short Story	Adventure	Animal
Number of Students	4	2	3	5

Draw a pictogram to show this. Use Key: ▭ = 2 students

6.

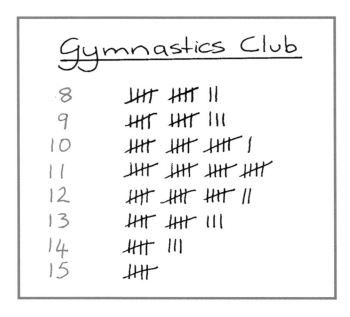

Gymnastics Club

8	ⵀⵀ ⵀⵀ ‖
9	ⵀⵀ ⵀⵀ ‖‖
10	ⵀⵀ ⵀⵀ ⵀⵀ ‖
11	ⵀⵀ ⵀⵀ ⵀⵀ ⵀⵀ
12	ⵀⵀ ⵀⵀ ⵀⵀ ‖‖
13	ⵀⵀ ⵀⵀ ‖‖‖
14	ⵀⵀ ‖‖‖
15	ⵀⵀ

Ayoko found out the ages of the people in her gymnastics club. This is her result sheet.

(a) Draw a pictogram for this. Make up your own key.

(b) "There are more 11-year-olds than 10-year-olds in this club," said Ayoko. Write 2 more sentences about your pictogram.

Review 1 Jessica asked some families how many days they spent on their summer holiday. She drew this pictogram.

No. of Days	Number of Families
Fewer than 7	○ ○
8	(
9	○ (
10	○ ○ ○
11	○
12	○ (
13	(
14	○
More than 14	○
	Key: ○ = 2 families

(a) How many families had fewer than 7 days holiday?

(b) How many families had 9 days holiday?

(c) How many families did Jessica ask altogether?

(d) How many families had more than 8 days but fewer than 14 days holiday?

(e) What else can you tell from this pictogram?

Review 2 This table shows the foods that students in Amelia's class liked. Draw a pictogram to show this. Use **Key** ǀ○ǀ = 2 students.

Foods Liked	
Food	Number
Potato	⊮⊦⊦ ⊮⊦⊦
Cabbage	⊮⊦⊦ |||
Tomato	⊮⊦⊦ ⊮⊦⊦ |||
Cucumber	⊮⊦⊦ ⊮⊦⊦	
Peas	⊮⊦⊦ ⊮⊦⊦ ||
Cauliflower	⊮⊦⊦ ||

PRACTICAL 14:4

Your Class

Find out some information about people in your class. You might find out about

       – favourite pop stars
       – month of birth
       – favourite colour
       – favourite animal
       – number of brothers and sisters

Draw pictograms to show your information.

Another Subject

Find out about something to do with one of your other subjects. You might choose

       – populations of countries
       – rainfall
       – sports results

Draw pictograms to show your information.

Outside

Collect information about your school grounds or nearby. You could collect information about

       – the types of trees growing
       – the colour of cars passing the
         school
       – the amount of rubbish left after
         lunch

Draw pictograms to show your information.

BAR GRAPHS

PRACTICAL AND DISCUSSION 14:5

- On a piece of paper write down the month you were born in. Go and stand or sit by the others in your class who were born in the same month.
  How could you show this information on a graph?
  Discuss.

- Brad's class decided to show their information on a graph like this.

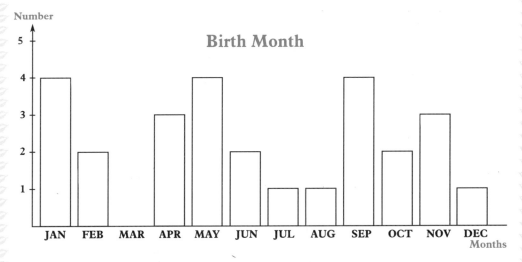

Discuss this graph. Do you think it is a good way of showing this information?

This type of graph is called a *bar chart* or *bar graph*. Why do you think it is called this? **Discuss.**

- "A bar chart should always have a title," said Awaz.

  What other things do you think a bar chart should always have? **Discuss.**

A **bar chart** or **bar graph** is often used to show the results collected on a tally chart and frequency table.

Example
This table shows the eye colour of people in Garth's class. These results are shown on the bar graph below.

Eye Colour	Tally	Number
Brown	卌 III	8
Blue	卌 卌 II	12
Green	卌	5
Hazel	III	3

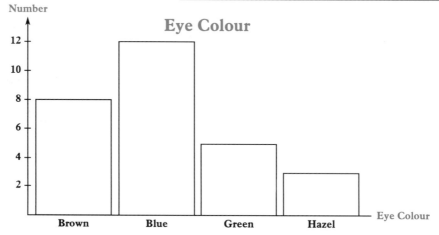

EXERCISE 14:6

1. Tania asked each of the students in her class how they got to school each day. The results are shown on this bar chart.

How many come to school

(a) by car

(b) by bus

(c) on foot

(d) by cycle

(e) by train?

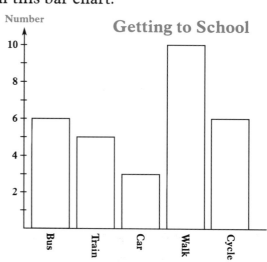

2.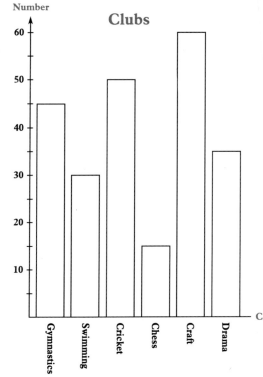

Number

Clubs

This bar chart shows the number of students who belong to the clubs at Greensward School.

(a) Which club has the most students?

(b) Which club has the fewest students?

(c) How many students belong to the gymnastics club?

(d) How many more students belong to the cricket club than the chess club?

(e) Which club has 30 students?

(f) What else does this graph tell you?

3.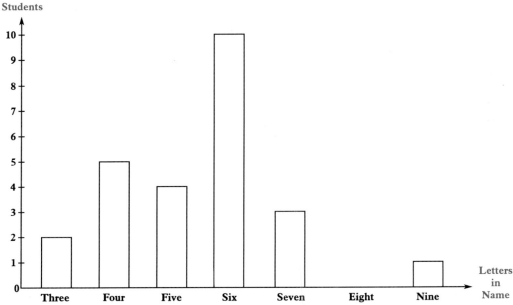

Number of Students

Letters in Name

Gordon wrote down the names of the students in his class. He counted the letters in each name and drew this bar chart.

(a) Copy and fill in this table.

Letters	Number of students
three	
four	
five	
six	
seven	
eight	
nine	

(b) How many students have five letters in their name?

(c) How many students are in Gordon's class?

4. This bar chart gives the number of times it rained on each day of the week from February to July one year.
Copy and finish the bar chart below.

Day	Number of times
Monday	8
Tuesday	10
Wednesday	6
Thursday	7
Friday	6
Saturday	8
Sunday	10

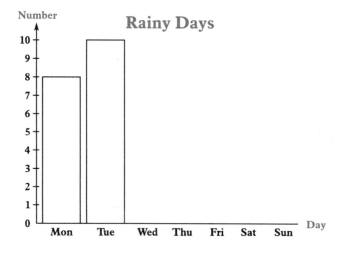

5.

Opinion	Number
Excellent	10
Very Good	8
Good	6
Not Very Good	0
Poor	1

Huda asked the others in her class their opinion of "Top of the Pops". The results are shown on this table.

Draw a bar graph to show these results. Put opinion along the bottom and number up the side.

6. This table shows the number of police call-outs in one week.

(a) Draw a bar chart to show these results.

(b) What does your graph tell you?

Day	No. of Call-Outs
Monday	18
Tuesday	10
Wednesday	25
Thursday	40
Friday	60
Saturday	85
Sunday	10

Review 1 This bar chart shows the number of children who got on the 0710 train from Sevenoaks.

(a) Which two days did the same number of children get on this train?

(b) How many children got on this train on Monday?

(c) How many children got on this train on Friday?

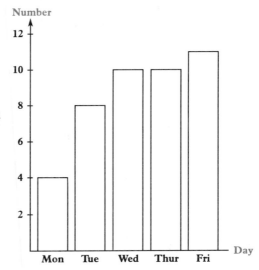

(d) On which day did 8 children get on the train?

(e) On which day did the greatest number of children get on the train?

Review 2 Gwilym asked his friends what party food they liked best. The results are shown in the table.
Draw a bar chart to show this. Put the party food along the bottom and the number of people up the side.

Party Food	Number
Pizza	4
Ice-cream	6
Chocolate Biscuits	3
Cake	1
Crisps	7
Jelly	5

PRACTICAL 14:7

● Choose a word that could have different endings added to it. Say the word to people in your class and ask them to put an ending on it.

Example

Snow _ _ _ _   **Book** _ _ _ _
   snowman   bookshop
   snowflake   bookmark
   snowdrop   bookworm

Draw a bar chart to show the results.

● Choose one of these to collect results about.

   – number of times a person steps on cracks when walking along a path
   – number of brothers and sisters people have
   – number of books of different types you own
   – midday temperatures each day this week
   – number of pets people own

Find a way of collecting the results. Show your results on a bar chart.

DISCUSSION 14:8

"I think pictograms show results better than bar charts," said Samantha.

"But bar charts are easier to read," said Derek.

Discuss what Samantha and Derek said.

INVESTIGATION 14:9

TOPIC

Choose a topic to investigate. Some ideas are

> food
> families
> another country

Investigate as much as you can about this topic. Present what you found on a poster, mural or booklet. Use pictograms and bar graphs.

WORK THIS OUT

The number of letters in a word is given on this chart. For instance there are two A's. Unjumble the letters to make a word.

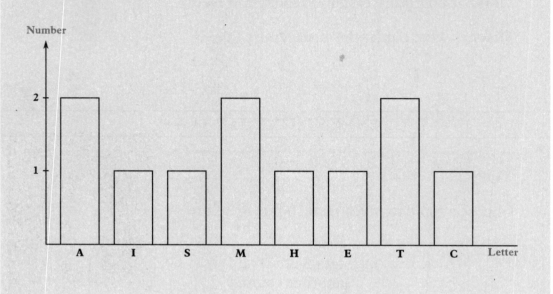

1.

Animal	Name	Age	Colour
Dog	Rufus	8	Black
Cat	Toby	2	Ginger
Cat	Dusky	$5\frac{1}{2}$	Black
Rabbit	Sniff	$2\frac{1}{2}$	White
Dog	Hoot	7	Gold
Cat	Clark	4	Black
Cat	Ziggy	2	Tabby

This table shows the information in a database.

(a)   Write down the names of the black animals.

(b)   Write down the names of the cats.

(c)   Write down the names of the animals that are older than 2.

(d)   How many black cats older than 2 are there?

2.

Day	Number of Tickets
Monday	⧈⧈⧈⧈⧈⧈⧈
Tuesday	⧈⧈⧈⧈⧈⦙
Wednesday	⧈⧈⧈⧈⧈
Thursday	⧈⧈⦙
Friday	⧈⧈⧈⧈⧈⧈⧈⧈⧈⧈
	Key: ⧈ = 2 tickets

This pictogram shows the number of tickets sold for the class raffle one week.

How many tickets were sold

(a)   on Monday

(b)   on Tuesday

(c)   on Thursday and Friday

(d)   altogether?

3. Manuel asked each student in his class which animal they liked best. The results are shown on this bar chart.

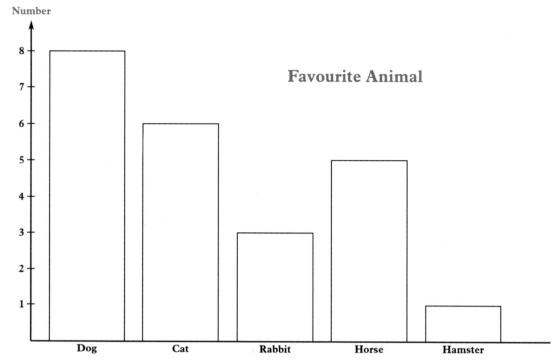

Favourite Animal

(a) Which animal is liked best?

(b) How many students like horses best?

(c) Which animal is liked best by 6 students?

(d) How many students did Manuel ask altogether?

4. This chart gives the times and heights (in metres) of high tides on one day.

HIGH TIDES								
TODAY	AM	HT	PM	HT	TODAY	AM	HT	PM	HT
London Bridge	11.54	6.4	-----	----	Liverpool	9.14	8.3	9.28	8.5
Aberdeen	11.34	3.8	11.43	3.8	Lowestoft	7.09	2.3	8.07	2.3
Avonmouth	4.57	11.3	5.22	11.6	Margate	9.52	4.3	10.28	4.4
Belfast	8.57	3.1	9.14	3.1	Milford Haven	4.07	6.0	4.27	6.2
Cardiff	4.42	10.5	5.07	10.8	Newquay	3.02	6.0	3.21	6.2
Devonport	3.26	4.8	3.44	4.9	Oban	3.36	3.4	4.00	3.7
Dover	8.58	5.9	9.25	5.9	Penzance	2.31	4.8	2.48	4.9
Falmouth	2.56	4.6	3.14	4.7	Portland	4.16	1.8	4.29	1.7
Glasgow	11.01	4.5	11.25	4.5	Portsmouth	9.10	4.4	9.33	4.2
Harwich	9.38	3.6	10.09	3.7	Shoreham	9.05	5.5	9.31	5.5
Holyhead	8.29	4.9	8.37	5.1	Southampton	9.02	4.1	9.19	4.0
Hull	4.06	6.5	4.41	6.5	Swansea	4.12	8.2	4.34	8.5
Ilfracombe	3.48	7.9	4.09	8.2	Tees	1.19	4.8	1.52	4.8
King's Lynn	4.09	5.6	4.44	5.7	W'lton-on-Nze	9.35	3.7	10.06	3.9
Leith	12.04	4.8	12.39	5.0					

(a) The morning high tide of 3.8 metres at Aberdeen was at 11.34 a.m. What time was the evening high tide?

(b) How high was the evening high tide at Aberdeen?

(c) What time was the morning high tide at Dover?

(d) How high was the evening high tide at Shoreham?

5. Mrs Wong made a list of the cakes she sold.

Fruit	5
Chocolate	12
Banana	7
Sponge	8
Apple	3

Copy and finish this pictogram.

Cake	Number Sold
Fruit	⬭ ⬭ ⊂
Chocolate	
Banana	
Sponge	
Apple	
	Key: ⬭ = 2 cakes

6. This chart shows how much it costs to send a letter.

    (a) How much does it cost to send a 150g letter by First Class mail?

    (b) How much more does it cost to send a 300g letter by First Class than by Second Class mail?

Weight not over	First Class	Second Class	Weight not over	First Class	Second Class
60g	25p	19p	500g	£1·25	98p
100g	38p	29p	600g	£1·55	£1·20
150g	47p	36p	700g	£1·90	£1·40
200g	57p	43p	750g	£2·05	£1·45
250g	67p	52p	800g	£2·15	**Not admissible over 750g**
300g	77p	61p	900g	£2·35	
350g	88p	70p	1000g	£2·50	
400g	£1·00	79p	Each extra 250g or part thereof 65p		
450g	£1·13	89p			

    (c) Anika sent a letter by Second Class mail. This cost £1·20. What is the greatest weight this letter could be?

    (d) How much would it cost to send a 275g letter by First Class mail?

7. Sonia wrote down what she saw at the circus.

    Copy and finish the bar graph on the next page.

What I saw	Number
Clowns	III
Horses	IHT III
Lions	IHT I
Monkeys	II
Dogs	IHT IHT
Tight Rope walkers	I

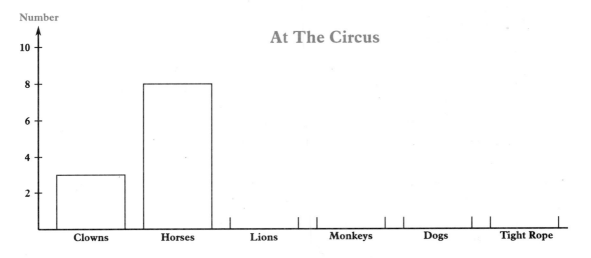

At The Circus

8. Anne asked the people in her mother's gardening club which flower plants they liked best. The results are shown on this table.

   Draw a pictogram. Use the Key ✿ = 2 people.

Plant	Number of people
Nemesia	8
Geranium	7
Pansy	15
Petunia	10
Lobelia	5

9. This table gives the number of runs made by each person in a class cricket team.

   Draw a bar graph for this information.

Name	Number of runs
David	7
Jessica	16
Shirin	12
Casey	9
Erin	10
Andrew	8
Megan	5
Bimla	8
Wendy	3
Tony	2
Peter	1

10. Christine ordered Christmas presents for her mother and father and her two sisters from a mail-order booklet. Copy and finish this order form.

Item	Code	Price (£)
Torch Keyring	228	---
Butterfly Bookmark	229	---
Big Badge Kit	---	---
Water Candles	---	---
	TOTAL	

 Torch Keyring
Press the button and a tiny light comes on to show you the keyhole. ***89p each***

 Butterfly Bookmark
A great way to mark your place — the butterfly clips onto your page. ***£1.50 each***

 Big Badge Kit
Create 8 jumbo badges just the way you want them! Kit contains pin-on badges, coloured discs, printed designs, lettering and felt pens. Fun to wear! Ages 6-14. ***£5.95 each***

 Water Candles
Candles in a flower design, which burn while floating on water (e.g. in a glass). Full instructions given. 5 to a pack. ***£1.99 set of 5***

 Weather House
A favourite — when the man comes out it is going to rain, and when his wife does it will be fine. ***£3.99 each***

11.

MONDAYS to FRIDAYS - DOWN

LONDON CANNON STREET Dep	12.43	..	13.13	..	..	13.43	..	..	14.13	..	..	..	14.43	..	..	..	..	15.13	..	..	..	15.43
London Bridge	12.47			13.47				14.47					15.47
LONDON VICTORIA . Dep	..	13.00		13.32	..	14.00	14.19	..	..	14.32	..		15.00	15.19	..	15.32	..	..	..
Orpington	13.03	13.24	13.32	..	14.03	14.24	14.32	..	15.03	15.24	15.32	..	16.03
SEVENOAKS Arr	13.12	13.34	13.42	14.01	14.12	14.34	14.42	15.01	15.12	15.34	15.42	16.01	16.12
Dep	13.12	13.34	13.42	14.02	14.12	14.34	14.42	15.02	15.12	15.34	15.42	16.02	16.12
Hildenborough	13.18		14.18		15.18		16.18
TONBRIDGE Arr	13.22	13.43	13.50	14.10	14.22	14.43	14.50	15.10	15.22	15.43	15.50	16.10	16.22
Dep	13.23	13.43	13.52	14.10	14.23	14.43	14.52	15.10	15.18	15.23	15.43	15.52	16.11	16.23
High Brooms	13.29	13.56	14.29	14.56	15.29	15.56	16.29
TUNBRIDGE WELLS Arr	13.32	14.02	14.32	15.02	15.32	16.02	16.32
Dep	13.33	14.02	14.33	15.02	15.33	16.02	16.33

(a) Rainer caught the train that leaves London Bridge at 12.47. What time did he arrive at Tunbridge Wells?

(b) Tony caught the 13.13 train from London Cannon Street. He got off at Orpington. Tony wanted to spend at least 2 hours at Orpington and then catch the next train to High Brooms. Which is the earliest train Tony should catch from Orpington?

(c) How many trains stop at London Victoria between 12 p.m. and 2.30 p.m. on Monday?

(d) A train arrives at Tonbridge at 14.22. What time did this train leave London Bridge?

12.

Class \ Hair Colour	Light Brown	Dark Brown	Mid Brown	Red	Black	Blonde	Totals
Mr Thom	4	5	7	2	5	3	
Ms Patel	2	5	8	0	3	6	
Mrs Young	6	2	6	3	7	2	
Totals							

Abbie collected information on the hair colour of the students in 3 classes at her school.

(a) How many of these students had Dark Brown hair?

(b) How many students were in Mr Thom's class?

(c) Copy the table. Add up the totals.
What number goes in the grey box?

(d) Write some statements about hair colour in these 3 classes.

INDEX